THE MAGHREB SINCE 1800

KNUT S. VIKØR

The Maghreb since 1800

A Short History

HURST & COMPANY, LONDON

First published in the United Kingdom in 2012 by
C. Hurst & Co. (Publishers) Ltd.,
41 Great Russell Street, London, WC1B 3PL

Printed in India

A Cataloguing-in-Publication data record for this book
is available from the British Library.

ISBN: 978–1849042246 (hardback)
978–1849042017 (paperback)

This book is printed using paper from registered sustainable
and managed sources.

www.hurstpub.co.uk

CONTENTS

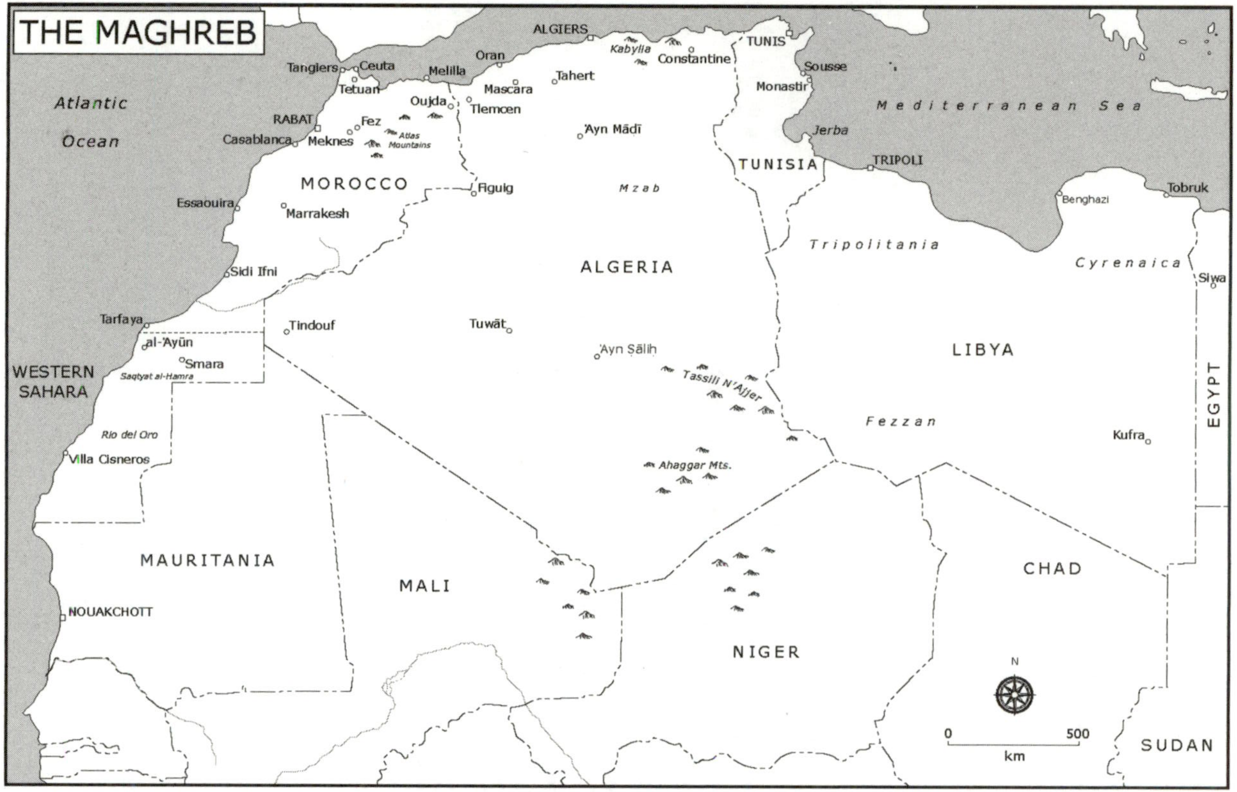
THE MAGHREB
Atlantic Ocean
Mediterranean Sea
Tangiers
Ceuta
Tetuan
Melilla
Oran
ALGIERS
Kabylia
Constantine
TUNIS
Sousse
Monastir
Jerba
TRIPOLI
Benghazi
Tobruk
Siwa
RABAT
Casablanca
Meknes
Fez
Oujda
Tlemcen
Mascara
Tahert
Atlas Mountains
'Ayn Mādī
Mzab
Figuig
MOROCCO
Essaouira
Marrakesh
Sidi Ifni
Tarfaya
Tindouf
Tuwāt
ALGERIA
TUNISIA
Tripolitania
Cyrenaica
LIBYA
EGYPT
'Ayn Ṣālih
Tassili N'Ajjer
Ahaggar Mts.
Fezzan
Kufra
al-'Ayūn
Smara
Saqiyat al-Hamra
WESTERN SAHARA
Rio del Oro
Villa Cisneros
MAURITANIA
NOUAKCHOTT
MALI
NIGER
CHAD
SUDAN
N
0
500
km

INTRODUCTION

In the spring of 2011, North Africa was suddenly at the forefront of global news. While the 'Arab Spring' soon spread to Yemen, Bahrain, Syria and elsewhere, it was often described as the 'events in North Africa', or 'in North Africa and the Middle East', reversing the normal order of the two elements. The reason was, of course, that the earliest events took place in Tunisia and Egypt, both on the North African side of the Arab world. This raises the question of what these geographic terms actually mean. While we intuitively know where the Middle East lies in the world, most of us will have problems in saying exactly where it begins and ends. Is Afghanistan part of the Middle East or not? The Sudan? And what about 'North Africa': is that part of the Middle East, or something separate?

The confusion spills over into academic literature. When you pick up a 'History of the Middle East', it will always include Syria, Palestine and Iran. But you have to look closer to see if it also deals with Algeria, Libya and Morocco. Sometimes it does, sometimes it does not, depending on how the author has defined the 'Middle East' of its title. And when they are included, the North African countries are often dealt with summarily. So there is a need to tell the history of this region, even though much of it is part of the general history of the Arabs and of the Islamic world, the larger entities to which it belongs.

But if the Moroccans and Tunisians are Arabs and Muslims, just like the Iraqis and Syrians, why are they set apart like this? If the 'Middle East' has no obvious geographic boundaries nor makes any intuitive sense as a name (middle between what?), why not include all the Arab countries in the term? Largely, that is the result of historical accident. The term is British and rooted in colonial history.[1] It was used to refer to the areas under British control and their immediate surroundings. Thus, the British-controlled North African country of Egypt is always part of 'the Middle East', but the countries under French dominance further west were of less concern to the English.

However, while it is true that the historical and cultural ties that bind all of the Arab world together are stronger than those that divide east from west, the distinction is not altogether a modern colonial invention. In Arabic, we have always had the same distinction between the *mashriq*, the land where the sun rises, and the *maghrib*, the land where it sets. The line of demarcation can largely be situated where the Sahara touches the Mediterranean at the bottom of the Bay of Sirte in central Libya; thus the *maghrib*, our Maghreb, consists primarily of the modern states of Libya, Tunisia, Algeria and Morocco.

The distinction is partly linguistic: the *maghribī* 'dialects' of Arabic are collectively so different from the eastern dialects as to make communication difficult or impossible. But it is also historical: the Maghreb was always far away from the centre of the Islamic empire, and often had its own history, partly as an ensemble, partly in separate entities. It was closer to Europe, and closer to sub-Saharan Africa than the eastern lands. Thus, while the Maghreb was always an integral and important part of the Islamic empire and the Muslim world, it was also very often a somewhat distant part.

It is thus the Maghreb rather than 'North Africa' that is our concern here. North Africa in geographic terms also includes Egypt and the new [North] Sudan, but these are not considered a part of the Maghreb, neither by language nor history. So 'North Africa' is also an ambiguous term: sometimes it includes

Egypt, Sudan and the Horn of Africa; at others, and perhaps more often, it is used synonymously with the Maghreb.

In the framework of regional 'Maghreb' cooperation, one or two other regions in the far west, Mauritania and/or Western Sahara, are often included. They become relevant to our history mostly in the recent, post-colonial period, and they will be dealt with primarily in that period.

In this little book, we will map out the history of this Maghreb with a focus on the last two centuries. It is a survey only, but we will try to locate some of the factors that unite the region and where we can easily compare countries, and those where they have parted ways. These provide different models, and from this we may see some of the background for the developments that take place today.

This book is an expanded translation of *Maghreb: Nordafrika etter 1800* (Oslo 2007, 2011). Produced in the course of the rapid transformations taking place in the 'Arab Spring', it is brought up to date to November 2011.

1

THE GROWTH OF THE MUSLIM MAGHREB

The Maghreb has been Muslim for more than thirteen centuries. The Caliph's Arab armies had already won over the native Berber groups in the middle of the seventh century, shortly after they had conquered Egypt. But the Caliph lost his grip over the region not much later. The Abbasid dynasty of Baghdad ruled over all of the Muslim world—except the west, where only some areas of the Maghreb were under the Caliph's effective control. This was thus the region of the Muslim world that first began to strike out on its own politically and gained an autonomy that it largely kept throughout its history.

But while mostly ruling themselves, the Maghrebis quickly became fully integrated into the Muslim world in culture and religion.[1] The majority of the population probably retained their Berber language and identity throughout the Middle Ages, but became part of an overall multi-ethnic Muslim cultural world that united all Muslim lands. From the eleventh or twelfth century, Arabs started to gain numerically through immigration or by Berber groups adopting the Arabic language and ethnicity. At the end of the Middle Ages, the balance between them may not have been far from what it is today: the majority claiming Arab identity while there are strong Berber-speaking minorities in Morocco and Algeria, and significant groups also in western Libya.

While they maintained their language, the Berbers, however, shed their former religious beliefs and adopted Islam totally and almost immediately. Thus, the Muslim armies that entered the Iberian peninsula from the early eighth century and settled there—sometimes with their flocks and families—were as much Berber as Arab, but distinctly Muslim with Arabs and Berbers working in concert.[2]

The Berber nature of early Islam in the Maghreb was an important reason why it was so often in revolt against the caliphate. In the middle of the eighth century, emissaries came from Oman with an alternative brand of the religion.[3] The Khārijī branch—later known as the Ibāḍīs—did not believe that the Caliph, the head of the empire, needed to be an Arab of the Quraysh tribe, as other Muslims held. The most capable pious Muslim should rule, whatever his lineage, they claimed. Berbers and other non-Arabs certainly found this to be a sympathetic idea. In the course of the eighth century, a number of Khārijī-inspired Berber rebellions took place in various parts of the Maghreb.[4] Ibāḍī city-states were set up in many of the important trading towns, the most important being the Rustamid state of Tahert (now in central Algeria), which ruled over most of the central Maghreb from 761 to 909. In Morocco, Sijilmāsa was a crucial centre of trade in gold and slaves from West Africa, and under Khārijī rule.

The rest of the Maghreb mostly escaped the Caliph's power as well. The city of Fez was founded in 808 by a descendant of the Prophet in revolt against the caliphate, based on what can perhaps be called nascent Shīʿism, stressing his legitimacy as an Alid member of the Prophet's family.[5] Only Tunis and its surroundings had a dynasty of governors, the Aghlabids, who were formally subservient to the Caliph (but even they were, in reality, fairly autonomous) and in religious agreement with Baghdad.[6] Across the Straits of Gibraltar, the Muslims of al-Andalus (Muslim Spain) also followed the Caliph in religion, but never in politics; their ruler was a refugee from the ousted Umayyad dynasty and took no orders from the usurpers in Baghdad.

The Maghrebi heyday of the now almost forgotten Ibāḍī branch of Islam only lasted until the beginning of the tenth century. Then, a new powerful force crushed the Rustamids and other Ibāḍī centres and forced the Ibāḍīs to retreat into the desert, where they sought refuge in some oases and highlands and have remained there until today, peacefully, and engaged mostly in trade.

The new force that came, however, was not the army of the Caliph of Baghdad but of a rival who wanted to be not just a new Caliph, but a different sort of ruler. He too was a descendant of the prophet Muḥammad through his daughter Fāṭima, and claimed the right to rule on the basis of this kinship. These most powerful of the early Shīʿī rulers were thus known as the Fatimids. They did not belong to the branch of Shīʿism that dominates today in Iran, Iraq and Lebanon—the Imāmīs (or 'Twelvers')—but to the earlier and now minority Ismāʿīlī branch. The Fatimids later became powerful in Egypt and Syria, but their history in the Maghreb was rather brief.[7] They set up their counter-caliphate in Tunis in 909, after having crushed Tahert and the other Ibāḍī cities. But only sixty years later they moved on to Egypt, which they conquered in 969. They left behind a dynasty of Berber-based governors in Tunis: the Zirids. These quickly became autonomous from the Fatimids, and two generations later formally broke with them and denounced the Shīʿī theology. Thus Fatimid rule in the Maghreb was mostly restricted to the first half of the tenth century, which is called the 'Shīʿī century' in Middle Eastern history.

By this time the Abbasid caliphate had lost all effective power, and each region of the great empire was left to fend for itself. In religion, the Ibāḍīs had been forced into retreat, and the Fatimid Shīʿīs did not stay long enough to have any lasting influence on the faith. Throughout the Muslim world, the mood was for consensus and consolidation of Islamic theology after the long and heated controversies of the formative period. A new sense of a 'common', or sunnī Islam grew. In the Maghreb, Tunis became a centre for such Sunnī theology, in close contact both with al-Andalus and with the intellectual centres of the east. Thus, after the Fatimids' departure, the period of religious experimentation was largely over, and the Maghreb became a solidly Sunnī region, and has remained so ever since.

Great powers of medieval Maghreb: Almoravids and Almohads

In spite of this, the Islamic Middle Ages saw more political-religious controversies in the Maghreb than did the east. In the Mashreq a series of sultans and sultanates took power in rapid succession in various regions from the twelfth to the sixteenth centuries. But after the fall of the Fatimids, religion and theology was never cause for military conflict among Muslims and hardly used as a rallying-cry for any would-be sultan; they all fought to preserve the same Sunnī order.

Not quite so in the Maghreb, where they would all now also consider themselves to be Sunnī, although but not in exactly the same fashion. In the early eleventh century, ʿAbd Allāh ibn Yāsīn (d. 1059) came to the Ṣanhāja Berber tribe in today's southern Morocco, and called for a *jihād* against any remaining Shīʿīs, Ibāḍīs and other heretics, and in favour of a literalist interpretation of the Revelation.[8] Under him and his successor, Ibn Tāshfīn (d. 1107), they brought most of the western Maghreb under their Ṣanhāja-based movement, which was called *al-Murābiṭūn*, or Almoravids in English. As al-Andalus was at that time in crisis and under pressure from Christian invaders from the north, the Iberians asked the Almoravids for help; a call they answered, but then took control over al-Andalus for themselves in the process. In the following three centuries, the political destinies of the Maghreb and Muslim Iberia were to be linked.

In the early twelfth century, however, the Almoravids were challenged by another Berber movement, this time based in the Maṣmūda tribe, the Almohads *(al-Muwaḥḥidūn)*.[9] Again this was a tribal movement for political overlordship, which also used theology to justify its struggle. Their leader, Ibn Tūmart (d. 1130), claimed to be the divinely inspired *mahdī*, the eschatological leader who is to lead Muslims at the Day of Judgement.[10] He also followed a literalist view of Islam, but of a different nature; he (alone in Muslim history) supported the 'externalist' interpretation of Islamic law called Ẓāhirism, which rejected human interpretation of the divine texts and would only accept the literal words of the Qur'ān and Sunna. This was more a theoretical than a practical position, and in reality both law and theology largely followed the Mālikī tradition that at this time had come to prevail in all of the Maghreb.

Like their predecessors, the Almohads ruled over both al-Andalus and the Maghreb, and in fact united the region as far east as Tripoli; they even faced and defeated some crusaders who had ventured into Tunis. Apart from the brief period of caliphal rule just after the Muslim conquest, this was probably the only time when all of the Maghreb was united under one single ruler. However, like their predecessors—and like most medieval dynasties—the Almohad's rule began to unravel after three or four generations, and by the middle of the thirteenth century they controlled only small areas in western Maghreb.

The fall of the Almohads marked the end of the formative period of the Muslim Maghreb. It had seen the rise and fall of a series of states, from small city-states to empires, with shifting borders that generally did not coincide in any way with those of today. Only the province of Ifrīqiya around Tunis could be said to have a specific and enduring identity, with local rulers from the Aghlabids in the eighth century to the Hafsids in the sixteenth. But the other early states, Rustamids, Fatimids, Almoravids or Almohads, all ruled either over bits and pieces of today's states, or over regions that cut freely across borders, some even across to the Iberian peninsula, and cannot be directly linked to any modern country in particular.

The formation of modern states

After the Almohads, the region went into a period of even greater chaos for two centuries, until a new pattern started to form where we can see the embryos of today's nations forming (or at least two of them, Morocco and Tunisia, the other two being defined perhaps more as the areas between Morocco and Tunis, and Tunis and Egypt respectively). Theology was then no longer an issue in political struggles here any more than in the Mashreq; all of the Arab world had come under the dominance of a uniform Sunnī theology, and while all rulers of course based their reign on the defence of the religion, promoting the lawful and forbidding the unlawful, they could not realistically claim that their adversaries were less orthodox than themselves.

The most enduring of the dynasties that grew out of the Almohad period was the Hafsids, originally an Almohad family of governors in Tunis who retained power over the town after the masters had disappeared, and kept it until the late sixteenth century.[11] The formal borders of 'Tunisia' were not yet established. The Hafsids could, at times, rule over areas considerably larger than today's state, while at other times they controlled only the town and its close surroundings, and at yet other times, not even that; the ruler of far-off Fez conquered Tunis twice in the mid-fourteenth century. Nevertheless, Tunis was clearly established as a political and cultural centre for a specific region known as Ifrīqiya, which was to become our Tunisia.

By this time, the Maghreb had come far in its transition from a Berber to an Arab region. An important stage in this process of Arabization was the invasion—or immigration—of Arab nomads, of whom the most famous were the Banū Ḥilāl of the eleventh century, followed by the Banu Sulaym and Banū Ḥassān.[12] These events are often described as the tipping point in the change. However, we also find that groups that were described as 'Berber tribes' in the early centuries appear as 'Arab tribes' half a millennium later. Thus, there was probably also a continuous process of transformation of ethnic identity by groups and individuals over the centuries, where more and more of the population came to see themselves as Arabs, whatever their genealogical origin.

Another profound transformation began further west, when the regions from the Atlas mountains down to the Atlantic coast, which had been central to the far-flung Almoravid and Almohad empires, began to coalesce into a separate country; a state that came to be known in Arabic as the 'farthest west' (*al-Maghrib al-Aqṣā*) and in English, Morocco. This process of 'nation formation', or perhaps 'country formation', took several centuries, but can be said to have begun under the Marinids, a dynasty of Zenata Berbers who toppled the last Almohad rulers in the mid-thirteenth century.[13] They did try, like their predecessors, to expand their rule over larger parts of the Maghreb—it was they who briefly conquered Tunis, and they maintained control over eastern towns like Constantine and Oran for some time, but they were more and more concentrated into the area that was to become Morocco. They made the northern city of Fez their capital, rather than the previous capital of Marrakesh (from which our name 'Morocco' is derived), and Fez was from that time the political centre of the country.

This was also the time when relations with the neighbours across the Gibraltar Strait changed. While the Marinids did make some incursions into Andalus, they were, unlike their predecessors, not interested in trying to control any regions there. Like most rulers of their time, they made deals and alliances across religious borders, often working with one Christian kingdom against another Muslim/Christian alliance. But by the end of the thirteenth century, Muslims had lost much of their ancient country of Andalus, retaining only a small stretch of land from Granada down to Malaga. Many of the inhabitants of Cordoba, Seville and the other Muslim towns fled or emigrated southwards to Morocco. This influx of Iberian Muslims profoundly influenced Moroccan society and culture, and one of the central quarters of the medieval city of Fez is still called 'Andalus'.

The Gibraltar Strait was no more a barrier for the Christians than it had been for the Muslims centuries before, and they pursued their luck southwards. The new kingdoms, Castille, Aragon and Portugal, raided Maghrebi coastal towns, occupied some and harassed the Muslim rulers or at least those with which they were not in temporary alliance. This exacerbated Christian-Muslim relations, and the old task of defending Muslim lands in Andalus turned into a task of defending Muslim lands in the Maghreb, a frontier that was to last until the twentieth century.

The Marinids, increasingly beset by internal troubles and unrest among the tribes, were not able to resist these incursions effectively. So, their grip on power weakened towards the end of the fifteenth century. At this time, Fez gained even more symbolic power when the remains of the city's founder, Idrīs, a descendant of the Prophet, were miraculously found in the city. But the Marinids did not have much time to draw the benefits of this. After a brief interlude, during which short-lived groups vied to take control, another tribal group from the south came to take the reins and institute a new kingdom.

However, while all the earlier dynasties had been Berber, the Saʿdīs, who by 1550 had defeated their rivals and secured the throne, claimed an Arab identity, and even more: they were *sharīfs*, descendants of the Prophet.[14] This gave them a special mission to rule the Muslim state, and this set the country apart from its neighbours. Thus, it helped forge a separate Moroccan identity, linking it to the rule of the Saʿdī dynasty.

The Saʿdīs were also able to make a strong defence against the Portuguese and forced them out of many of the strongholds they had established on the Moroccan coast. But new forces blocked any expansion towards the east. Instead, the Saʿdīs turned south. Perhaps the greatest of the Saʿdī rulers, Aḥmad al-Manṣūr (1578–1603), sent an army across the Sahara desert in 1592 and conquered the great West African empire of Songhay, bringing back both gold and African scholars.[15] But in spite of this short-lived excursion south, the most noticeable aspect of the Saʿdī state was that it, for the first time, established an area for the dynasty that survived their own demise, unlike the medieval circulation of dynasties that each created for themselves a region according to whatever strength or inclination they had. By liberating 'polity' from 'dynasty', increasingly with an idea that the country was an entity in its own right, we can say that a geographic 'Morocco' had started to emerge.

However, the fall of the Saʿdī dynasty did not follow long after its greatest hour; already on al-Manṣūr's death his successors fell into fighting over the spoils and tribes began again to carve out their own pockets of autonomy. Some of them also used Islamic frameworks. Sufi brotherhoods had by this time become very important in the Maghreb, forging bonds with tribal leaders or across tribal lines.[16] Most of them had no political ambitions, but some had played a part in politics, not least influenced by the Saʿdīs' claim to religious legitimacy. When that dynasty had gone, some Sufi shaykhs, who were also tribal leaders, formed a small state, the Dilāʾīya tribe/brotherhood, which controlled much of Morocco for a short period around 1640.

But by the late 1660s a new family had come to power, and it was to end the rotation of dynasties: it is still the ruling family of Morocco today, the oldest dynasty in the Arab world and one of the oldest in the world. Like the Saʿdīs, they could well use a religious legitimacy in the face of the Sufis, so they also claim to be *sharīfs* of the Prophet's family through Fāṭima and ʿAlī. From this, they are known as the ʿAlawī dynasty. The strength and stability of the new dynasty owed much to the efforts of sultan Mawlay Ismāʿīl (1672–1727).[17] He sought to forge a strong central state. To support it, he imported African slave soldiers, who became known as the *bukhārī* soldiers, and who were to be loyal to him alone and not to one or other of the divisive tribes with which earlier rulers had to deal.[18] Ismāʿīl made his capital at Mèknes, a town not far from Fez but still so distant that it could balance the two major centres of Morocco, Fez in the north and Marrakesh in the south. He dealt with the European powers, both in diplomacy and trade, trying to free the coastal towns that some of them still possessed. He also began a *jihād al-baḥr*, the *jihād* of the sea, which the Europeans, not incorrectly, called piracy: those European nations or companies who did not pay protection money to the sultan had their ships boarded, their goods taken and their passengers sold into slavery; most Europeans found it better to pay.[19]

After Ismāʿīl's death, his successors found what other sultans raising slave armies have often found: their instrument turned against them. The *bukhārī* soldiers became a dominant political power in their own right and began imposing their will on the sultans. This caused dissensions with Fez, which was dominated by religious scholars who had always opposed the *bukhārī*. The town struggled for autonomy, while the sultans again had to seek alliances with various Arab or Berber tribes to balance the power of the *bukhārī*. Thus, the old pattern remained: when a strong sultan ruled, the tribes accepted his power and paid their taxes and dues; but when the sultan was weak, they sought autonomy, either rebelling against the central power or negotiating their support for a price.

Autonomy under Ottoman rule

The ʿAlawīs thus inherited the territory and the geographical identity of the Saʿdīs; they were, without doubt, sultans of something called 'Morocco'. On their eastern border they faced a new world power that had emerged, and that in the early years had threatened to gobble up the new Moroccan entity: the Ottomans.

The Ottomans, who had been established in Anatolia from the fourteenth century, exploded into the Arab world at the beginning of the sixteenth. Damascus and Syria fell to them in 1516, and Cairo the following year. They continued their rapid advance westwards, and were in control of Algiers ten years later.[20] This was, however, as far as their lines of communication would go, and perhaps even a bit too far: their control over these western regions were for long periods little more than a formality. Thus, Algiers was not so much conquered by as donated to the Turks. The coastal regions between Tunis and Morocco had not had any centralized rule after the fall of the Almohads three centuries earlier, but had been contested between rulers in Morocco and Tunis and local pretenders, and were under increasing pressure from Christian naval forces. Culturally, the western part looked towards Fez, with the town of Tlemcen always a bone of contention between the sultans and local rulers such as the Zayyanids, who governed the town for long periods. In the east, the town of Constantine mostly fell under the influence of Tunis, but often escaping its political control.

Spain was also a nuisance on the Mediterranean coast. They occupied various port cities: both Oran in the west and Tripoli in the east. Muslim forces were eventually able to push them out, but Oran remained under Spanish control for two centuries until 1791. Thus the *jihād al-baḥr* was important, but was often left to adventurers of dubious credentials who set themselves up as warlords in towns that were outside the control of central Muslim powers. The most successful of them were two brothers of Greek origin: Urūj, who was killed outside Tlemcen in 1518; and Khayr al-Dīn, known as 'redbeard' or Barbarossa. He established himself in 1516 in the then insignificant village of Algiers and made it his headquarters.

When the Ottomans had demonstrated their power in the east, Khayr al-Dīn approached them and sought their favour as a useful ally. The Ottomans approved and, by making Khayr al-Dīn their admiral, gained control over his domains around Algiers. Both this outpost and his naval forces were important for them in their naval conflicts with Spain. To support their advance base at Algiers, however, they also needed control of the coast in between. Thus Ottomans with corsair support (or vice versa) took Tripoli in 1551, and from there made several attempts to capture Tunis. It changed hands several times between Spanish and Ottoman forces, until the Ottomans finally secured their rule in 1574, and then had command over all the southern Mediterranean coast east of Oran.[21]

While the Ottomans had thus united most of Maghreb's Mediterranean coast under a single authority, their mastery of it was, at least in the first two centuries, fairly uncertain. They established a border with Morocco by capturing Tlemcen in 1551, while the Spanish-controlled Oran was a buffer on the coast. They also made forays into Morocco, but were repulsed by the Saʿdī sultans, who, by keeping them out, became virtually the only remaining independent Arab rulers in an otherwise Ottoman-ruled world. It is not clear how serious Ottoman intentions on Morocco were, and what control they could have hoped to have held in this very distant land, but in any case, the Ottoman–Moroccan border remained relatively stable over the centuries that followed.

The Ottoman influence was strongest on the coast. In the interior, tribes or local religious leaders ruled with little outside interference until the nineteenth century.[22] At times, ambitious governors could venture south to impose taxes or settle scores, but their main interest there was the continuity of trade across the Sahara. Some trade routes passed through southern Morocco, others across regions such as the Fezzan (now south-western Libya), or desert towns like Ghat and Ghadames in the centre-east and the Tuwat and Mzab oases in the west. These desert trading towns were, in effect, independent city-states throughout the period: some of them under the control of the Ibāḍīs who had found refuge there, others under local leaders who kept peace and order so that the beneficial trade could continue. As long as it did, the powers on the coast were mostly satisfied.

After establishing their power, the Ottoman central authorities seemed more or less to lose interest in the Maghreb as time went on. They set up Ottoman state structures, more developed and bureaucratic than those known in the medieval period, and divided their Maghrebi lands into entities that were to become foundations for the future. Thus, they designated three towns, Algiers, Tunis and Tripoli, as centres of administration and organized the territories around them. Tripoli had formerly been under Hafsid control, but was now to be administered separately from Tunis. Constantine, long within Tunis's sphere of influence, was also removed from their charge and attached instead to Algiers.[23]

The Ottomans appointed Turkish pashas to administer these regions, and brought in professional Ottoman soldiers—the elite Janissary corps—to help them.[24] However, the Janissaries soon established themselves as local independent rulers, often in conflict with the pashas and other local forces. Under their commanding officer, the *dey*, the Janissaires became the real power-holders in both Algiers and Tunis throughout much of the seventeenth century. This shared background, however, did not prevent the rulers of the two towns from fighting each other. Tunis and Algiers became bitter rivals for the supremacy of the Ottoman west. The central authorities in Istanbul did little to stop the rivalries—and wars—between the two or to impose any real control. From the late sixteenth century on, all these 'regencies', as they were called, were in fact autonomous under the rule of shifting alliances of Turkish soldiers and officials: Janissaries under *dey*s, or other strongmen with titles such as pasha or bey.

The elites of all these provinces were thus of Turkish origin and spoke Turkish. The Arabic and Berber population in the countryside interested them mainly as possible subjects for taxation, but in general they could not be bothered—or find it efficient—to collect the taxes themselves. Instead, they made arrangements with selected tribes, who collected taxes as far as they were able, evidently for a price. These tribes became known as the *makhzan*, 'tax office' (or 'state') tribes, and were given special privileges; their leaders, *qāʾid*s, became notables who were largely autonomous from the capital as long as they were able to deliver the taxes expected from their territory.

The corsair business flourished, and most European powers signed treaties that formalized payment of dues to the various masters along the coast, in return for being left in peace. In Tunis, an alliance of Turks under a bey eventually allied with local Arab groups and wrested power from the dominant Janissaries in the mid-seventeenth century, which stabilized the power in the province. Then, in 1705, the very capable Ḥusayn Bey came to power. He strengthened the state and founded a stable dynasty that was to reign in Tunis for more than 250 years, until the establishment of the republic in 1957.[25]

In Tripoli, the eighteenth century also saw the establishment of a durable dynasty of rulers, when Aḥmad Qaramānlī took power in 1711.[26] He ruled with the help of a new class of *qulloghli*, people of mixed Arab and Turkish descent. In the Ottoman class society, this was a group separate and inferior to the true Turks, but helped the Qaramānlīs keep power in their province for more than a century, and become more localized. Thus, Arabic replaced Turkish as the main language of administration in the mid-eighteenth century. Technically, Tripoli's rule also extended towards Cyrenaica, the largely desert areas east of the Bay of Syrte, where the Ottomans established a centre at Benghazi. However, Tripoli's attempts at actual control over these remote regions were only intermittent, and, like the inland tribes, the Cyrenaicans outside the few coastal towns there mostly ruled themselves.

Early reform

Towards the end of the eighteenth century, however, there were many indications of a crisis in the Ottoman regions. Over time, the balance of strength in the Mediterranean had begun to tip in favour of the Europeans. Evidently, they had no wish to continue paying the unwelcome protection money to the Muslim corsairs any longer than necessary. So they began to renege on or not renew their deals with the corsairs, preferring instead to protect their ships with arms. This cut seriously into the income of the Barbary states. Some of the provinces had an alternative income from the trans-Saharan trade from Africa, which was still considerable in spite of increasing competition from European ships which traded on the West African coast.[27] Algiers, however, had little such income and not much else to look for in terms of an economic basis, and the *dey*'s rule was tottering. But the need for economic reform became more and more evident in the other provinces as well, alongside the necessity to strengthen their military forces in the face of the European challenge.

Reform was also on the agenda in sections of society that were not concerned with Europe—politics or the military. Debates on religion and Islam grew out of the Islamic intellectual traditions, and continued discussions that had been raised over centuries. After the unification of theology on a common Sunnī basis at the end of the medieval period, the main lines of the religious sciences had been established. There were, however, always discussions about details and interpretations of these general lines. Nevertheless, many voices in various parts of the Islamic world began to warn against complacency in religious thought, and that the words of the great medieval authorities in theology had begun to overshadow the need for the intellectual discovery of the original sources of religion.[28] Such voices, which had been heard earlier, became more vocal in the eighteenth century, and in particular in religious centres away from Istanbul and Cairo. Here, the Maghreb came to host several such trends for religious reform. Since the medieval period, two of the most important centres of Islamic learning were in the Maghreb: the mosque-universities of Zaytūna in Tunisia, and the Qarawīyīn in Fez, which vie with each other (and with the Azhar of Cairo) over the claim of being the oldest university in the world.[29] Both educated many major religious scholars and were centres of discussion and development.

These discussions were quite unrelated to the political powers of the day. Sultans or other state authorities should not get involved in religious matters. The sultan may well be a 'commander of the faithful', but it was ingrained in the religious scholars' view that political power was anathema to religious purity, as any application of power by necessity entailed oppression (*ẓulm*) of someone or other, and was certainly a diversion from the correct path—that was the nature of politics. Thus, the sultan should protect the Muslim community and its law, but he should leave the discussion of religious matters to the specialists, the religious scholars.

But some sultans were genuinely interested in religion. Sultan Muḥammad III of Morocco (1757–90) had been able to stabilize the ʿAlawī's power and restored a stable and relatively peaceful reign to the country.[30] He also had deep scholarly interests and even wrote books on theology, and was accepted into the community of scholars on those terms. He argued strongly for religious reform, and criticized the ossification of Islamic knowledge that he felt had taken place over the preceding centuries. In particular, he attacked the view that neither scholars nor laypeople should read the original sources of Islam, such as the Traditions of the Prophet (*ḥadīth*), and certainly not interpret them. Many religious authorities insisted that latter-day scholars should content themselves with secondary commentaries on the early texts, or even just the commentaries on the commentaries. These, the traditional opinion held, were sufficient; today's scholars should not bother their heads with trying to understand the originals. The sultan and other reformists felt that such a view cut the believer's and scholars' link to the Revelation and must lead many astray. In his capacity as sultan, Muḥammad intervened in the university and forbade the reading of most of these comments. Instead he promoted the distribution of the original *ḥadīth* collections, in particular the most prestigious of these, that of al-Bukhārī, which had hardly been read in Morocco in the last centuries.

The sultan was not alone in this view. There was a tradition of reform that grew among the religious classes at the Qarawīyīn university at Fez. Many agreed with reformers in the Mashreq, such as the Wahhābīs in Arabia, that the religion must return to its roots and free itself from 'blind imitation' of traditional scholarship. But they disagreed with the violence with which the Wahhābīs spread their ideas, and that they called Muslims who disagreed with them infidels.[31] The work for reform must be done peacefully and gradually. Other Maghrebi scholars, such as those of the Zaytūna university in Tunisia, rejected the Wahhābī suggestions and condemned them and their ideas outright. The reform ideas were thus stronger in Morocco, but pre-dated the

Wahhābī upsurge and were neither initiated nor to any great degree influenced by them.

When this discussion came up, Sīdī Muḥammad had already died, in 1790. After the customary period of unrest following a sultan's death, it was a younger son, Mawlāy Sulaymān, who ascended the throne.[32] He was, like his father, as much interested in religion as in politics, and followed his father's ideas of reform. However, he rescinded some of the most radical religious decrees his father had made. Both these two ʿAlawī sultans were thus involved in reform, but their emphasis was on an *Islamic* reform inspired from within, rather than the social and economic reform ideas spurred by European modernism that their successors were to promote.

Mawlāy Sulaymān was less successful than his father at keeping peace in the country. A series of revolts marked his rule, from Berber tribes and in Fez and other major cities. Sufi brotherhoods were also important in these events, as they had been before, and the young Darqāwī order provided a link between the Berber and the urban protests.[33] They were also involved in an attempt at expansion. The Moroccan sultans had always had their eye on Tlemcen, just across the Ottoman border, and the citizens of the town had vacillated between welcoming and rebuffing them. In 1804 they rebelled against the Ottoman *dey*, and under the leadership of the Darqāwīs asked the sultan to claim the city for Morocco. Although tempted, Sulaymān decided against a war with the *dey* and instead put the Darqāwī leader in prison. But the episode was yet another sign of the weakness of the *dey*'s rule over his province.

Tunisia had, for much of the eighteenth century, been harassed by Algiers, which had often been the stronger of the two towns. Towards the end of the century, a vigorous Ḥusaynid ruler, Ḥammūda Bey (1782–1814), was able to bring Algiers' domination to an end and re-establish Tunis as master of its own territory.[34] But he saw that there were deeper reasons for the weakness of his country, and he was the first ruler we may call a modernist reformer in North Africa. He made efforts to promote reform in agriculture and to create a more balanced economy. However, like so many of those that followed, his greatest concern was with the military and to strengthen the army.

This first bout of reforms turned out to be short-lived. After Ḥammūda's death, his successors soon dropped these efforts. They also had little control over the state's expenditures, and tried to cover the growing shortfall in income by imposing harsh taxes, in particular on agriculture. But this did not bring in enough money, and to cover the deficit they began to take out loans from European creditors. Thus, the Europeans, who had only recently been objects of Tunisian corsairs, now became important economic partners and soon came to gain an influence over Tunisia's economic affairs. Their main interest was in 'opening' the North African markets for European goods and traders, by getting rid of the Bey's state monopolies over the country's external trade. By establishing economic partnerships with the Bey, and partly also by playing off the various North African rulers against each other, they were able to promote their interests further.

In Tripolitania, the early nineteenth century also saw a strong and capable, if brutal, ruler in Yūsuf al-Qaramānlī (1795–1832).[35] He too sought cooperation and partnerships with European interests, and allowed them to gain influence. Tripoli was particularly important as the entrepôt of the trans-Saharan trade route to Lake Chad, which was the most prosperous route at this period. However, Tripoli did not have full control over the route, which passed through the Fezzan region before entering the Sahara. The Fezzan had been autonomous since the fifteenth century, living off the transit trade. It did not suit al-Qaramānlī to be dependent on others, and in 1812 he staged a coup in Fezzan that removed its traditional ruler and imposed one of his allies on the throne. This started a period of troubles that were to cost the trade route dearly.

Tribal unrest was not uncommon in the regions under Qaramānlī rule. Cyrenaica in the east, an area in which the Qaramānlīs had virtually no interest, had even seen a full-scale tribal war in 1832, without Tripoli caring much about it. But there were troubles closer to home, in Tripolitania proper, that were of greater concern. A tribe (or rather, a confederacy of tribes), the Awlād Sulaymān, was particularly rebellious, and revolted again and again. The Qaramānlī forces were able to defeat them in 1818, but in 1831 they rose again. This time they went south to the Fezzan, toppled Qaramānlī's man, and took control over the region and thus over the lucrative trade route. He could not dislodge them, and losing control over this region weakened his position, at the same time as the European interests in Tripoli grew ever more powerful.[36]

Although the Qaramānlī pashas had, like the beys of Tunis and *deys* of Algiers, in reality been independent rulers, they were technically servants of the distant sultan of Istanbul. He had not involved himself directly in the affairs of his North African domains for centuries, but now he found the occasion prudent to reassert some control. Thus in 1835 an Ottoman army was sent to Tripolitania and took charge. The Qaramānlīs were removed, and direct rule from Istanbul was imposed. Once Tripolitania proper was under their control, they sent an army southwards to Fezzan, and in 1842 expelled the rebellious Awlād Sulaymān Bedouins forcibly from the region.[37] The tribe fled south across the desert and settled in the region of Kanem (in Chad today). That did not, however, make them less rebellious, and hardly less of a nuisance. They made it their business to harass and raid the trading caravans that passed through the area, making it generally unsafe to travel there. The unrest caused major disruptions for trade, and was an important contributing factor to the decline of this trade route over Fezzan to Tripoli at the end of the century.

The route was soon replaced by a new trade route that opened further east, which had as its terminus Cyrenaica, the 'half empty' area that few rulers before had cared about. The Ottomans were not too concerned either, but they were an orderly people and included it in their administrative structure as a 'sub-province', *mutṣarrafiya*. They made the small town of

Benghazi its administrative centre, and the town also profited from the new trade route that came to use it as its northern terminus. However, Ottoman authority hardly stretched outside the coastal strip, and the nomads in the interior remained masters in their realm. Hardly any attempts were made to force them to pay taxes or follow commands from their administrators on the coast.

2

THE FRENCH INVASION OF ALGERIA

In the course of the nineteenth century, Europeans slowly began to gain influence over economic affairs both in Tunis and in Tripoli by financing the activities of the beys and pashas.[1] In return, they suggested that they should be allowed into the local markets, and they sent 'advisors' to help whenever one of the rulers began a project of modernization or development. But they did not challenge the power of the sultan, bey or pasha directly.

The one big exception was the province that we must call by the name the French gave it, from 1830: Algeria, the Ottoman province between Morocco and Tunisia that had until then been very loosely ruled from Algiers. This was not the first time that the French had invaded an Arab country; Napoleon had taken Egypt just a generation earlier. But that was only a brief episode of three years' duration, even though it made Muslim rulers shudder and make plans for military reform. In Algeria, the French did not leave; they remained for more than one hundred and thirty years.

The conquest of Algiers is therefore often presented as the starting point for European 'colonial power' in the Middle East. However, this was not how it seemed at the time, and it was most probably also far from the imagination of those who gave the order. Rather, the conquest should be described as a failed punitive expedition. The French 'stumbled into' Algeria and were not able to find a decent way to leave, so they stayed.[2]

It all began with a quarrel about a loan. France owed the *Dey* a few million francs, through some intermediaries, and the *Dey* was pressing them to start paying up. When he suspected that the French were procrastinating to get out of paying, the debate got heated, and at a meeting on the matter in 1827 the *Dey* struck the French consul with a fly-whisk (or a fan). This was an insult to the honour of France, and the injury was not lessened when the *Dey* refused to apologize, and instead suggested that the French did something to pay the money they owed.

As it happened, 1830 was an election year in France, and it struck the government in Paris that it might be useful to show strength abroad before the election. So, they sent a naval force south to Algiers to punish the *Dey* for his insult. The expedition scored a rapid and total victory: the *Dey* capitulated even before the French ships could open fire. Even further, his whole government and regime just fell apart, leaving a power vacuum in the city and province. At the same time, something unexpected happened back in France—the July revolution of that year toppled the king and his government. The new power in Paris had more important things to worry about than the naval party in far-away Algiers, and the latter were largely left to their own designs as to what do to now. The original idea had been merely to teach the insolent *Dey* a lesson, or at most replace him with another and properly chastened *Dey*, and then head for home. But no replacement *Dey* could be found, and there was pretty much no government for him to rule even if they found one. Thus, several French generals saw this as a great opportunity to further the glory of France by hanging on to this new land that they had conquered so heroically, or rather, that had fallen into their lap.

There was no consensus on this view, neither among the military nor in the new government in Paris. Instead, the government looked for some ways to rid itself of the problem and get out of Algeria.[3] It was not able to locate anyone from the old *Dey* class who could serve as a ruler, and it would in any case perhaps not give a terribly good impression if France were to insert another of the old 'pirate chiefs' as ruler. So instead France turned to Algeria's neighbours and asked if any were interested in taking charge of the territory. Mostly, they were not. The Sultan in Istanbul, technically the supreme ruler of the region, had no wish to get involved. Muḥammad ʿAlī, the reformer of Egypt, was asked if he would like Algeria, but since his heart was set on Syria, he declined.

Only the *Dey*'s old rival in Tunis, Ḥusayn Bey, showed any interest. The French offered him control over both Constantine, which until 1598 had been considered part of Tunis's sphere of interest, and Oran in the west, a formerly Spanish territory which was closer to Morocco. Ḥusayn Bey sent his brother Muṣṭafā til Constantine, and his nephew Aḥmad to Oran. However, they soon discovered that the French had promised more than they could deliver. The French had indeed been to Oran and planted their flag there, but had left soon after and had no control in the town. In Constantine, the former Ottoman (or rather, autonomous) Bey was still in place and had not seen any Frenchmen around who could give his land away. He refused to go, and the Tunisians did not insist. They were not going to make war on behalf of the French, and went home.

The Moroccans did have an interest in what went on in Algeria, and in particular in the border regions. Their desire for Tlemcen was well established, and the leaders of the town again invited the Sultan to come and take control of the city. He did send a company to take the town but, like the Tunisians in Constantine, he found the gates locked.[4] A group of Turkish and *qulogh li* soldiers had established themselves in the town's citadel, and refused to surrender to the Moroccans. Thus, the Sultan pulled his forces back, and gave up the attempt.

However, he did want to signal that Morocco had an interest in this region, so he turned to one of the local leaders who had supported the Moroccan claim, and asked him continue the struggle in the Sultan's name. This man, who accepted the charge, was called Muḥyī 'l-Dīn al-Qādirī.

Muḥyī 'l-Dīn was first and foremost a religious Sufi leader, who had been influential in spreading the Qādirīya brotherhood in this region. But in the course of this religious activity, he had gained influence over some of the local tribes who sought his advice and accepted his counsel. He knew he could count on them to support his combat. The Qādirīya is probably the largest and most widespread of all Sufi brotherhoods, with branches almost everywhere in the Muslim world. It is not, however, a very strictly organized or hierarchical order. It should be seen more as a shared religious view, or a 'method' (the literal meaning of *ṭarīqa*, brotherhood) to reach the mystical goal of experiencing the divine. Organizationally, each lodge or *shaykh* is fairly independent, based on the personal authority of its shaykh.

Muḥyī 'l-Dīn had thus gained personal and spiritual authority through his efforts to build this brotherhood in western Algeria, but could not count on any structured organization that could help in this new, worldly, effort at combating the French. He was also more than 70 years old, and knew he could not himself lead the fight. Instead, he pointed to his son, ʿAbd al-Qādir, and asked the tribes and others who flocked to the cause to give their allegiance to him instead.[5]

ʿAbd al-Qādir was, by this time, about 25 years old, and clearly a very talented young man. He was to lead one of the most enduring resistance movements in the history of the Middle East, and also gained renown as a worthy opponent by many in France. He was not just a military man; he was also a religious scholar and Sufi, and left behind literary works, both religious texts and poetry, which gained him a stature separate from his political legacy.

Now, however, the order of the day was worldly affairs. ʿAbd al-Qādir exploited the political vacuum in western Algeria while the French were trying to find their feet on the coast.[6] He captured Tlemcen and the town of Mascara, making the latter his capital. This showed his capacity as a military leader, and he could ask for, and get, the allegiance of all the tribes in the region. Some, however, were more reluctant than others. Those who had worked as tax collectors for the *deys*, the *makhzan* tribes, were less enthusiastic and disliked the fact that the privileged position they had enjoyed was now taken over by the tribes that stood closest to ʿAbd al-Qādir. They gave their support to his struggle, but did not put much effort into it.

Today, ʿAbd al-Qādir serves as a national symbol for Algeria. But he himself had hardly any clear conception of this 'nation'. His base and his primary focus were his native western part of Algeria. In the east, the former Ottoman governor, Aḥmad Bey, was still in power and had established himself as an independent and efficient ruler of his region. ʿAbd al-Qādir saw him as an equal, and as long as Aḥmad Bey could keep up the anti-French front, ʿAbd al-Qādir saw no reason and had no ambition to become the ruler of all of 'Algeria'.

His relations with Morocco were also fairly confused.[7] His father, Muḥyī 'l-Dīn, had accepted to work as the Sultan's representative, and ʿAbd al-Qādir maintained this language, repeatedly saying that everything he did was as the envoy and on behalf of the sultan in Fez. Thus, the territory he held in Algeria was part of the Moroccan sultan's lands. But at the same time, and apparently without seeing the contradiction, ʿAbd al-Qādir called himself the *amīr al-muʾminīn* when speaking to his own people: the same 'caliphal' title that the Moroccan Sultan used, which indicated that ʿAbd al-Qādir considered himself the sovereign ruler of his lands. This was also the reality; the Sultan had no actual control and little influence over ʿAbd al-Qādir's actions and strategies.

In fact, when ʿAbd al-Qādir stood at the apogee of his power, there were many in Morocco who would rather see the relation inversed—that ʿAbd al-Qādir should depose the Sultan and make himself the master over all of Morocco. ʿAbd al-Qādir himself did not give any indication that he had such ambitions, but that the idea was floated at all demonstrates that the relationship between the 'nations' of Morocco and (western) Algeria was rather porous in this period.

The French were, at this time, contained in the coastal areas, in particular the areas around Algiers and Oran. They did not have the strength to challenge either ʿAbd al-Qādir's western nor Aḥmad Bey's eastern provinces, and took a cautious attitude. Instead of attacking ʿAbd al-Qādir, they signed a treaty with him in 1834, drawing up some lines between their respective areas of influence.[8] The contents of this treaty were ambiguous, as it was written in two different versions: one French and other in Arabic, with significantly different content. The French governor in Algiers made sure that Paris did not find out about the Arabic version, because this text acknowledged ʿAbd al-Qādir's right to rule over all of western Algeria. It would cause a severe rebuke from the government at home if they realized that the local governor had accepted this, but it was, in fact, only an acknowledgement of the actual situation on the ground.

However, not all French generals in Algiers were happy with this policy of 'limited occupation', and strove to extend their territory. They sought an alliance with the *makhzan* tribes, those who had only reluctantly joined ʿAbd al-Qādir's cause. Two of these tribes broke away and sought the protection of the French, who accepted this charge. This was a clear violation of the treaty, and was intended by the generals as a declaration of war. It thus led to the first active campaign between ʿAbd al-Qādir and the French, in 1835.

ʿAbd al-Qādir was simultaneously engaged in creating a new state structure from his capital in Mascara. Notwithstanding his classical and Sufi background, he sought a rather reformist and modern model for his statelet, influenced to a large degree by the *tanẓīmāt* reform ideas of Istanbul and of Muḥammad ʿAlī of Egypt. Thus, he established a *niẓāmī* army composed of regular sections and with a structured officer corps. But when the fighting erupted in 1835, this new structure was still only in the process of formation, and his core military strength remained the tribes of the region who had declared their allegiance to him and fought in their traditional manner.

This was not sufficient to face up to the French forces, and the French captured both the towns that ʿAbd al-Qādir controlled: Mascara and Tlemcen. However, the French command was still working within the policy of limited occupation, and did not have enough soldiers to hold on to these towns of the interior over any extended period of time. So they hoped, in vain, that the campaign itself was enough to break down the support for ʿAbd al-Qādir's cause, and withdrew from both towns after a few weeks. ʿAbd al-Qādir was thus able to return and took up residence again after only a short period; he continued with his state-building project while consolidating his military hold over the areas under his control.

Thus, this first fairly brief conflict did not change much for either side, and moves were made to renew the original agreement between them. A new treaty was signed at Tafna in 1837. Again, this was formulated in two versions which differed in content, and again the Arab version recognized ʿAbd al-Qādir's territory. This time he was even allowed greater areas: now all of central Algeria, south of the French-controlled sector on the coast, was acknowledged as belonging to ʿAbd al-Qādir, including large territories over which neither side had, at that point, taken actual control. The treaty did not include Constantine and its regions in the east, where Aḥmad Bey still ruled. ʿAbd al-Qādir did, however, emphasize how important it was for him that there was a Muslim ruler in Constantine. A French attempt to extend their power over that region would be considered inimical, and ʿAbd al-Qādir would in that case return to war.

Both parties realized that the Tafna agreement could not be a permanent solution: it was no more than a temporary halt that would allow each of them to build up their strength for the inevitable showdown. ʿAbd al-Qādir used the time to consolidate power in his territories. While he kept the local *makhzan* tribes as channels of state power, he also established a modernized administrative system, dividing his state into regions. The model that he established was to endure, in that the French would later maintain the system he created until 1871.

He also sought to strengthen his political position by eliminating pockets of internal dissent. Thus, he spent considerable time trying to control a rival Sufi brotherhood, the Tijānīya, which had its centre in the oasis of ʿAyn Māḍī in the Sahara.[9] The Tijānīs had not been politically active, and ʿAbd al-Qādir's personal affiliation to his Qādirīya order was, as mentioned, not very important in his actual political and state-building efforts. Nevertheless, the Tijānīs had refused to recognize his authority, partly no doubt because of *ṭarīqa* jealousy; they would not bow to a ruler from the Qādirīya. Thus they were potential rivals, and ʿAbd al-Qādir sent a large force into the desert and laid siege to ʿAyn Māḍī, but it took several months before the Tijānīs finally gave in.

While this was going on in the south, the French had been active on the coast. They began to expand towards the east. While their first campaign against Constantine was somewhat a failure, they persevered and forced Aḥmad Bey to flee in the autumn of 1837, before again leaving the region. This was exactly what ʿAbd al-Qādir had warned against. He reiterated his demand and was more specific: if the French tried to establish a French-controlled corridor between Constantine and Algiers, which meant they would permanently occupy this region, that would be a declaration of war and ʿAbd al-Qādir would be forced to reopen hostilities. The French ignored his protest, and in 1839 sent a force to keep the road between the two towns open. ʿAbd al-Qādir responded as he had promised by attacking the French forces in the west.

However, the French had now moved away from the 'limitations' in their occupation. It had been General Bugeaud who had championed this reserved attitude and who was the architect of the Tafna treaty. But now, having been made Governor, he had come to the conclusion that the conflict could only end with one party winning permanently over the other, and that the French now had sufficient forces to be that winning party.

He thus struck hard against ʿAbd al-Qādir's still mixed and unformed army, and re-took the two towns of Mascara and

Tlemcen in 1841–2. This time, however, they did not pull back again. ʿAbd al-Qādir had thus lost the seat of his state and government and was forced to change from conventional battles to guerrilla warfare, backed by the tribes' superior knowledge of the region. He created a 'moveable tent capital', the *zmala*, where as much as possible of his administrative apparatus was moved continuously to stay out of reach of the French attackers.[10] As the French still did not have the manpower to maintain continuous control over all the territory they gained, ʿAbd al-Qādir was able to keep them at bay for several years, always moving his *zmala* and his forces to regions where the French were absent. Thus, for the first two years, his guerrilla campaign was fairly successful.

Nevertheless, time appeared to be on the side of the French, who pressed always closer to ʿAbd al-Qādir, due not least to some gruesome massacres of local villagers who could have supported the resistance. Thus, in 1843, he had to move the *zmala* across the border into Morocco, using it as a hinterland from which his moveable units could make guerrilla raids into the French territories.

In this way, Morocco was brought into the conflict. So far, sultan ʿAbd al-Raḥmān (1822–59) had stayed out of it, in spite of his early pronouncements that ʿAbd al-Qādir was his 'representative'; he had limited his support for the *jihād* to verbal statements only. It was, however, an important part of his legitimacy as *amīr al-muʾminīn*, commander of the faithful, that he protect the Muslim community from foreign invaders. Moroccans had certainly had enough experience of these over the centuries, as victims of regular attacks on their coastal cities from both Spain and Portugal. So, the Moroccan sultan had promoted his share of 'sea *jihād*' corsairing but, like the Regency powers further east, he had found this to be less profitable in the last half century or more.[11]

Thus, it had been most welcome that he could fulfil his obligation of *jihād* against foreign invaders by giving enthusiastic, but only verbal, support for ʿAbd al-Qādir's war; and he had been less than happy with the peace treaties that ʿAbd al-Qādir had signed, without of course at any time consulting him. The Sultan would rather have preferred a more steadfast and principled resistance than waffling with strategic compromises. But as long as ʿAbd al-Qādir stayed sagely on his side of the border, these minor disagreements could be ignored, and the sultan wholeheartedly supported the effort.

It was an altogether different matter when ʿAbd al-Qādir crossed with the bulk of his forces into Morocco proper. Then the Sultan was suddenly in danger of being caught between two options, neither of which was enviable.

On the one hand, not many years had passed since the last rebellion against his predecessor Mawlāy Sulaymān, and he could never be sure that public opinion, that is opinion among the potentially rebellious tribes or towns, would not turn against him as well. ʿAbd al-Qādir was immensely popular in his struggle, in particular in eastern Morocco where tribal and family links bound much of the population to those fighting in ʿAbd al-Qādir's war. So, it would be dangerous for the Sultan to be perceived as vacillating in his support for the resistance.

On the other hand, it was obvious that the French were now a major military force to be reckoned with. They respected the borderline with Morocco, but only as long as the Sultan did so as well. They made it abundantly clear that any active support from the Sultan's side to ʿAbd al-Qādir would be met with a stern reaction. They also tried to pressure him into halting his verbal support, but the Sultan could with some justification argue that this would only lead to his own overthrow. There were, as mentioned, already voices that would like to see ʿAbd al-Qādir himself on the Sultan's throne, and a popular rebellion for ʿAbd al-Qādir was a distinct possibility with which neither the Sultan nor the French would be happy.

No such rebellion transpired, and ʿAbd al-Qādir had probably never entertained any idea of marching on Fez; he had enough on his plate. But in order to strengthen his position in the war, he had to provoke the Moroccans into a more active supporting role. There was little use in asking the Sultan, so instead he began to agitate among the Moroccan soldiers in the border town of Oujda [Wujda] in northern Morocco, and was able to convince some of them to join him in an attack on a French post across the border.

This turned out to be a bad idea from the Moroccan point of view. The French saw here a clear proof that Morocco had joined ʿAbd al-Qādir's cause, and responded by bombarding two Moroccan ports, Tangier in the north and Essaouira in the south. The Moroccans were unable to respond to these naval attacks. At the same time, French troops crossed the border and occupied Oujda. The Sultan gathered an imposing army, including parts of the new and modernized forces he had been building up. However, the army turned out to be poorly trained and ineptly led, and was crushed by the French forces at the battle of Isly (1844). The French then withdrew in the secure knowledge that the Sultan had learned his lesson.[12]

This was in fact the case. While the Sultan continued to make pious statements in favour of ʿAbd al-Qādir, he decided it was too dangerous to allow him to remain in Morocco, and demanded that he move back to his own territory. ʿAbd al-Qādir himself, and his active forces, had in fact gone back and forth and made attacks inside Algeria, but there were no longer any permanently safe areas there for his *zmala*. So he kept them on the Moroccan side, and the relations with the Sultan became uglier when the *zmala*'s leader executed some French prisoners who had been brought into Morocco. The Sultan declared ʿAbd al-Qādir a rebel for not having followed his orders, and sent a force against him. However, some of the soldiers refused to fight against ʿAbd al-Qādir, who was thus able to overcome the Moroccans.

Nevertheless, he was in a very difficult position, squeezed between the Moroccan soldiers on one side and the French on the other. He did not have the strength to fight on both fronts at the same time, and his forces dwindled rapidly. In the end his choice was only between which side to surrender to, the Moroccans or the French. He chose the latter, and gave himself up to the French in December 1847, after fifteen years of alternating resistance and state-building. He was imprisoned first in southern France, then a few years later deported to Damascus, where he lived out his days as an author and religious scholar, near the international centre of the Qādirīya brotherhood.

3

THE MAGHREB BECOMES FRENCH

1850–1912

The resistance to the French did not end with ʿAbd al-Qādir. As the French moved southwards and eastwards from the established coastal regions, they were met with numerous rebellions and attempts to stop them. But these efforts were mostly local and did not significantly hamper the French expansion. Thus, by the mid 1850s they had de facto military control over all of Algeria.

It was the French occupation that made the territories between Tlemcen and the Tunisian border into a unified 'Algeria'. ʿAbd al-Qādir had never gained a foothold in the east, and the tribes of that region reacted more according to their own local context than to the situation in the far west.[1] But from mid-century onwards, the new country had, more and more, a shared destiny, as the French either were not aware of, or did not care about, the differences that existed between the west and the east of Algeria.[2] Their administration was to be the same, even if the social structures to be administered were quite different from region to region.

Thus, while it is convenient for an historian to treat the Maghreb before 1830 as a single unit, although with some differences between Morocco and the Ottoman-ruled provinces, the French conquest of the middle section of the Maghreb makes it easier to see it as four separate stories: alongside Algeria in the middle, Morocco under its Sultan to its west, Tunisia under the Bey to its east, and Tripolitania under direct Ottoman rule beyond Tunisia. But in the century that followed, the developments of the two regions to the west and east, Morocco and Tunisia, began to follow some parallels that make it useful to see those two countries as one strand of modern Maghrebi history, while the two others, Algeria and Tripolitania (later Libya), share some other similarities that can perhaps constitute a different strand.

The two nations of Algeria

Of the four, it is however Algeria which has the most unique story, not just in a Maghrebi context, but in all of modern Middle East history. We tend to speak of the European domination of this region as 'colonial rule', but hardly any part of the Middle East was technically run as 'colonies' in the manner of sub-Saharan Africa, where Europeans most often imposed their will directly through colonial officers.[3] In the Middle East, it was more common that the traditional rulers, the sultans, shaykhs, beys, or what there might be, retained their formal sovereignty, while the Europeans were the real powers, often without any formal status as a 'protector' of what was then named a 'protectorate', not a colony.

This may also be what the French had in mind for Algeria in 1830, but if so, they had been unable to achieve it. They were stuck with a large—including the desert regions, a huge—territory with a largely hostile population, but without the benefit of a local upper class or formal ruler that could function as a buffer against popular hostility. But they were not willing to consider Algeria a 'colony' either. Instead, they quickly decreed that it was now an integral part of France. It should become a region, a *département*, just as Bretagne or Picardie—a France across the sea from Marseilles.

In order to become French, however, it had to be populated by Frenchmen and women. Inclusive as the French notion of nationality might be, they did not consider letting the local Arabs or Berbers become French. Thus, a French population must be imported to their new lands.[4] The government started up a programme of recruiting Europeans to emigrate to Algeria. A very useful occasion for this presented itself in 1848 with the defeat of the February revolution of that year. The former revolutionaries were given the choice between prison and deportation, or to be welcomed as new citizens of Algeria where they would generously be given land and allowed to cultivate the earth. Many chose the latter option, and so became *colons*, not 'colonial masters', but ordinary people who came to settle and build a future for themselves and their descendants in a new and virgin France.

These not quite voluntary settlers were joined by enthusiastic volunteers. Many of the newcomers were utopian socialists who saw this as an opportunity to create a new society according to their ideals from the ground up, free from the social and political strictures of the homeland, a kind of French America in Africa. Unfortunately, they were better as thinkers than as farmers. Most of them, including the urban revolutionaries from 1848, had little or no background in or knowledge of agriculture. The lands the authorities gave them had been purchased or confiscated from local owners, and were mostly small and unproductive plots. The colonists did not have the experience or even the prospect of making a living out of these. After twenty years, most of the farms had been abandoned and the settlers had moved to the towns or, if they could, back to metropolitan France.

Nevertheless, new immigrants came to Algeria, and they were what, above all, was to distinguish Algeria from the other countries in the Arab world. The Europeans were always a minority compared to the local Arabs and Berbers, but when they reached one million at the turn of the century, they did constitute about one fifth of the total population of Algeria. Even if both Morocco and Tunisia received considerable numbers of French immigrants later in the century, these were never so many, nor had such great impact both politically and socially, as the *colons* in Algeria.

Not all these immigrants came from France. In fact, more probably came from Italy, Spain and other Mediterranean countries, and this at some periods caused some ethnic tensions between the settler groups. But, by the end of the century, most of them had assimilated into a homogeneous body of Algerian French, and they did start to see themselves as a separate body, distinct from the French of the mainland. Some even started to talk of Algeria as a separate nation, that is *French* Algeria, not of course including the Muslims. It may thus even be said that an 'Algerian nationalism' first grew among the *colons*, where the most extreme began talking of freedom from France in order to rule their own country without interference from Paris.

The aim of this autonomy would not have been to improve relations with the original inhabitants, the Muslims.[5] On the contrary, their irritation with Paris was, then as later, directed at whatever half-hearted concessions the central government made to the Muslims. The settlers were united in their opposition to any attempt at improving conditions for the Arabs or Berbers; any plan for development was blocked. This may sound like a harsh judgement, but it became one of the main fault-lines of French policy throughout their time in Algeria: what concern should the French have for the situation of the local Muslim inhabitants? It is very hard to find any answer among the settlers save 'none'. This total lack of compromise was clearly one important reason why Algeria's history took the dramatic turns it did in the French period, and this affected the course of events even later.

In the first generation of French rule, the issue took the form of a conflict between proponents of 'civilian' and 'military' rule. The occupation was, of course, initially military, and the army kept overall control as long as the danger of local revolts remained. But the increasing number of civilian settlers began to demand that they should be able to run their own affairs. The country was therefore divided into a 'military' and a 'civilian' zone, based on the importance of the civilian European population. This also became an economic as well as an environmental divide, as the Europeans expanded their agricultural interests and came to take over the best and most fertile and economically valuable regions. Thus, the civilian part became *l'Algérie utile*, the useful (or exploitable) Algeria.

There was no disagreement between the *colons* and the authorities about the expansion of European agriculture: both saw it as natural that the purpose of French rule was to 'create value' by the French exploiting the best land in the best way. More and more land was transferred to French ownership in the course of the century, through a variety of methods. Some was bought, some was confiscated from 'rebellious' tribes or otherwise.[6] The French also exploited a loophole in their own interpretation of Islamic law. The Ottoman Sultan had, for centuries, maintained the theoretical position that he, representing the state, was the actual owner of all cultivated land, and thus had the right to ask for tax or rent from the users. As he had ceded state authority to the French, they concluded that they were thus the rightful owners of all Muslim land, and thus free to distribute it as they wished. That the sultan did not have any such rights to redistribution—his theoretical ownership did not concern the *usufruct* or the right to exploit the land, only to tax it—was conveniently overlooked. One of these redistributions alone, in 1845, concerned 420,000 acres, of which the original owners retained 29,000, and the rest was given to the French. Through these and similar methods, more than 18 million acres of the most fertile land in Algeria was transferred to European owners.[7]

This division between military and civilian zones lasted until 1870. In the military zone, it was the army's understanding of the need for security and control that was the basis for government. And, perhaps surprisingly, this led to a much more understanding attitude towards the locals; it was in many ways the military that came to be the protagonist for Arab and Berber interests, as long as the army had any influence over Algeria.

This did not necessarily stem from a liberal attitude on their part, but from greater realism about the situation in the Muslim areas. The European population was still, in the 1850s and 1860s, a very small minority in a large territory that could hardly be said to be fully 'pacified'. The civilians lived in their own zone where they were in control, and they could to some degree ignore these demographic facts. For the military, however, it seemed unwise to provoke more unrest among the Muslims than was necessary. Further, in their paternalist and security-conscious way, they were also far better informed about Muslim society and culture than were the civilians, who saw nothing of interest there. The military administration established *bureaux arabes* or Arab offices, which were in charge of the administration of the Arab regions in the military zone. Their staff learned Arabic and studied the societies they worked in; much of what we know today of nineteenth-century Algerian Islam comes from their studies.[8] They came to believe that it was beneficial to maintain and utilize as much of the existing social structure as possible and only change what was required to maintain French control. The civilians therefore looked upon these offices with distrust as 'pro-Arab' and an impediment to the extension of their control over the land.

There was thus a basic mistrust and opposition between the military, and in particular the *bureaux arabes*, and the civilian European population. Many of the latter were Saint-Simonian socialists from France with a strong secular and anti-clerical background. They saw the *bureaux'* defence of Arab and Muslim culture as reactionary and bowing to an obscurantism that must cede before reason and civilization. The central government in Paris vacillated between these two positions, and was viewed with suspicion by both sides, but particularly by the settlers. When Napoléon III in 1863–1865 proposed some reforms aimed at according to the Muslims the status of 'French subjects' (without civil rights, of course), the settlers reacted strongly. This was not improved by the Emperor's offhand remark in a speech that Algeria 'is, of course, their country'.

In the end, it was the civilians who won. The French army lost the war with Germany in 1870–1871, and with it Alsace and Lorraine. Their honour was so soiled by this that they were unable to maintain their position in Algeria. It was not helped by the Berbers of Kabylia rising to the last great rebellion in 1871, under Muḥammad al-Mukranī. While the rebellion was defeated, it was proof that the military's strategy of appeasement had not been able to remove the danger of revolt. So, the settlers' demand for disbanding the two-zone system was granted, and Algeria became one single territory under civilian rule. Their system was to be only one, and it was the civilians who were to run it.

That did not bode well for the Muslims. Civilian rule did not of course mean civil rights for them. Instead, the new administration imposed new laws on the Muslims due to the 'danger of revolts'. These 'native laws' (*le code de l'indigénat*) largely removed all legal protection from Muslims. They did not have the right to move, they could be forcibly expelled or transferred, and lacked most other basic rights. All legal systems and local structures that had been maintained under the *bureaux* were abolished, and the French administration was the only local power. The Muslims were subservient to French laws, except in so far as the *indigénat* had taken away from them the rights that were accorded to French subjects.

The result was a near total destruction of the Arab society. In 1830, many of the cities of the region had developed an urban culture with trade and handicrafts, religious intellectuals and schools. By the end of the century, this was all gone. Towns like Algiers, Oran and Constantine had become European in architecture and economy. The Arabs who remained had been forced into the margins of European society, as labourers or servants. At the same time, there was a large influx of people from the countryside who had lost their land and joined the stock of cheap labour in the towns.

Many of the traditional social structures had also disappeared, tribes had been dissolved or left leaderless, and notables and other potential leaders lost their positions and social power. The *bureaux* had allowed Muslim schools to continue to educate religious scholars, but these schools were closed down by the civilian authorities, and no new ones were established in their place. Attempts by the central government to develop 'suitable' education for the Muslim population were effectively sabotaged by the settlers, and few such schools were established.

In spite of the extensive transfer of cultivable land to the Europeans, few of them were in fact engaged in farming at first. But the land turned out to be very suitable for viniculture, and this led to an upsurge for the agricultural sector. The smaller units were merged into large plantations, and wine became Algeria's main export. The landowners often resided in the towns, while the labour was left to Arab agricultural workers. Thus, the European society remained to a large extent an urban society.

The settlers did not make much distinction between the two major sections of the original inhabitants, the Arabs and the Berbers. However, some scholars and officials began to consider that the Berbers were the 'autochthonous' inhabitants of the country (while the Arabs were mere late arrivals) and that the Berbers were more 'white' and racially, marginally, closer to the Europeans. Since this conception made them in some way less Muslim than the Arabs, some small attempts were made to favour the Berbers and their main population area, Kabylia. However, this distinction did not have much basis in reality. The last great rebellion in 1871 had been among Kabyle Berbers, and since they were still subject to most of the same forms of discrimination as the Arabs, their attitudes were hardly more pro-French than those of the Arabs.[9]

Another group was, however, able to cross over the distinction from 'non-European' to 'European'. There had always been Jewish communities in the major Algerian towns, as elsewhere in the Arab world. They had an urban culture distinct from the Muslim one, and many were part of networks across the Mediterranean, but they had for centuries been an integral part of the traditional societies of the region. Towards the end of the nineteenth century, however, as the traditional urban culture was in the process of disintegration, the Jewish communities had been able to adapt culturally to the new European urban society, not least through their connections to Jewish communities in France. Probably with such support, the Algerian Jews were successful in obtaining the status of French citizens in 1870, and thus became part of European society. This sparked considerable resistance from the settler communities, who saw the Jews as 'Orientals'. An upsurge of anti-Semitic sentiment flourished in the wake of the Dreyfus affair in France, and in 1898 settlers organized widespread anti-Jewish riots in Algeria. It was at this time that the idea of separation from France was voiced among the most radical settlers. Their protests failed, and the laws granting citizenship to Jews remained. However, anti-Jewish attitudes remained in much of the settler community, and could be seen even after the horrors of World War II.

Morocco: hesitant reforms

The battle of Isly in 1844 was a wake-up call for Sultan ʿAbd al-Raḥmān.[10] He had already made efforts to strengthen and modernize his military forces, but the army had at Isly still fought under the traditional, and fairly inept, leadership of his brother and had not been able to put up any significant resistance to the French invaders. The Sultan thus began a forced programme of military reform and began, as ʿAbd al-Qādir had before him, to establish a *niẓāmī* army on the Ottoman model.

It took fifteen years before these reforms were put to the test. Shortly after ʿAbd al-Raḥmān's death in 1859, Spain attacked. The Spanish had always had an interest in the southern shore of the Mediterranean, not least because they had for some centuries controlled a few small enclaves on the Moroccan coast. After a change in government in Madrid, they felt it would boost their morale to have a small war in the south, and thus sent an army across the straits to occupy Morocco's largest Mediterranean town, Tetuan. It turned out that the Sultan's new army did not fare much better than his old one: they were unable to resist even this fairly middle-ranging European power. Thus, Morocco had to turn to diplomacy. Britain stepped in and negotiated a treaty that made the Spanish withdraw from Tetuan in 1861.

But their withdrawal did not come cheaply. Morocco had to pay an enormous war reparation to Spain, a debt that was to cause problems for the sultanate for decades. In addition, it had to cede the territory of Santa Cruz de Mar Pequeña in exchange for Tetuan. As it happened, neither party had any clear idea where this 'Santa Cruz' really lay, or if there even was such a place; but as late as 1934, the Spanish decided that the name referred to a small desert area called Sidi Ifni and so took control of it, according to the then 70-year-old treaty. It was only in 1969 that this last remnant of the 1861 war settlement was returned to Moroccan control.

It was very significant that it was a European power which thus stepped in and secured, after a fashion, Moroccan interests against another European power. From then on, Europeans became dominant actors in fashioning Morocco's future, and in particular its foreign policy.[11] To a large extent, the sultanate became an object of great power rivalry between the European powers, particularly Britain and France, who both had economic as well as strategic interests in the country. But other powers also made their interests known: apart from Spain, Germany later also stated a claim.

The Europeans also began to meddle in Morocco's internal affairs, and the reparations act with Spain, which Morocco had great difficulty in paying, proved an excellent opportunity. The main interest of the foreigners was to open up Morocco to European trade. They wanted free access to Morocco's internal market, but the country was also still an important outlet for trans-Saharan trade caravans.[12] The Europeans had for a long time traded in the goods brought from the south, but the sultans had severely limited their direct access to the markets in order to keep the trade under their control and thus draw benefits from it. The Europeans were restricted to certain coastal towns, and the Sultan reserved trade of particular types of goods for himself, his family or his favourites. This gave him the power to direct revenue to families or to groups that sought his favour in exchange for loyalty to him. But it also meant, of course, that other families or clans that were out of favour lost out economically, and these complained against the system, joining the protestations of the Europeans who also saw the monopolies as detrimental to their interests. Thus, the British had for a long time pressured the Sultan for access to markets, and he had in 1856 been forced to ease up on the restrictions. After the Madrid agreements in 1861, the influence of the British evidently increased, and the Sultan had to extend the access to Moroccan markets for both British and other European traders.[13]

In spite of this, the Europeans still preferred to trade indirectly through middle-men, partly due to culture and language, partly because the Europeans generally preferred to remain on the coast. These middle-men thus became important for the Europeans, and they made the Sultan accord privileges to these protégés, as the middle-men were called. They became, like the Europeans themselves, exempt from prosecution in Moroccan courts, and from taxes. Many protégés even took foreign citizenship, and the protégé position could be inherited within their families.

While this was beneficial for trade, the system soon degenerated. Europeans began selling protégé status to the highest bidders, in large numbers. Soon there were thousands of such protégé families, who thus bought themselves tax exemption and legal immunity. Most of them had no interest in trade nor participated in it, and many had never even met the European 'partners' with whom they were supposed to have a protected relation. This turned into a major problem for the Sultan, because it divided Moroccan society into two classes along quite haphazard lines, completely subservient to the inclinations of the various European consuls and traders.

The Madrid treaty also gave Spain the right to control the collection of the war reparation by manning the customs offices in Morocco. This led to a modernization of the administration, but under foreign control. Other Europeans, in particular the French, also began to invade the customs offices as well as other parts of the government administration in Morocco, under the cover of supervising the various treaties the country had made with the European powers.

The Sultan was, however, still in charge of forging domestic politics. The state's control over the tribal areas far from the capital had always been tenuous and dependent on the strength of the individual sultan and his ability to balance the various forces at hand. From the 1860s on, some tribal leaders in the south of the country began to strengthen their power by taking control over neighbouring tribes and thus creating larger units. They could potentially become dangerous rivals for the central government. The sultans of the period, both Muḥammad IV, who had succeeded ʿAbd al-Raḥmān in 1859, and his son Ḥasan, who came to power in 1873, preferred to use diplomacy to sort this out.[14] They established preferential relations with some of the dominant tribal leaders and appointed them as *qāʾids*, or local representatives of the Sultan. This ensured the basic loyalty of the chosen leaders: the *qāʾid* had pretty much a free hand in his own territory, but he did not challenge the Sultan's power directly. In exchange, he got the Sultan's support against his local rivals. These were thus induced to accept the authority of the *qāʾid*, who was in any case the strongest tribal leader in each region. This worked out well for both the Sultan and the *qāʾid*s and removed the danger of local rebellions against the central government. Perhaps the greatest of these *qāʾid* families was the Glāwīs, who were to play a crucial role in Moroccan politics for most of the coming century.[15]

With the support of and finance from the European powers, the Sultan also continued a policy of reform and modernization of the Moroccan economy. As always, however, his greatest concern was a credible military strength, and he continued to build a *niẓāmī* army and strengthen it with modern weapons and extended garrisons. This thus became the most important element of his reform programme.

Moreover, the economy went into a crisis towards the end of the nineteenth century, and was followed by a political crisis when the efficient Sultan Ḥasan died in 1894 and was succeeded by his 13-year-old son, ʿAbd al-ʿAzīz. In the first few years, when the latter was still a minor, the country was in the capable hands of Ḥasan's *wazīr*, Bā Aḥmad, who continued the policies of the old sultan and was able to keep conflicting interests in balance.[16] But when he died in 1900 and ʿAbd al-ʿAzīz took personal power, critics started to complain about the young Sultan's lack of experience and his extravagant lifestyle.

As it happened, ʿAbd al-ʿAzīz turned out to be a capable sultan who was keenly concerned with continuing the reform programme. But he lacked his father's ability to deal with the *qāʾid*s and other power centres and to play them off each other so as to give himself room to manoeuvre. Most of the *qāʾid*s saw him as young and weak and pushed to promote their own interests. Rivalries between tribes and families of notables grew stronger, with less and less regard for the result of this infighting for the country. There was also among the people a growing frustration with European influence and the way that the legal and economic systems discriminated in favour of the foreigners. However, as the Sultan had fallen more and more into debt with the European creditors, he had less and less influence over economic policy. It was in fact the balance of power between England and France that determined what should happen at the Sultan's court.

These two world powers were at this time in intense rivalry over possessions and influence, and Morocco was one of their bones of contention. England had traditionally had a strong interest in Morocco, and the British consul had been the most influential foreign advisor to the Sultan for most of the century. But Algeria gave France a long land border with Morocco, so that neither of the two European powers wanted to give the other the upper hand in how Morocco was to be run. Other European powers such as Spain had to be satisfied with playing second fiddle behind the two great powers, and the German attempt to join the fray was unsuccessful. But it was this rivalry between the powers that let Morocco remain an independent monarchy for as long as it did.

However, when England and France ended their rivalry with the *Entente* agreement in 1904, time was running out for independent Morocco. The two powers reached an understanding over how to divide their Middle Eastern interests: France accepted British control over Egypt, in exchange for getting a free hand in Morocco. Then, it was just a matter of time before the right occasion presented itself for imposition of French authority.

The events that led to the takeover started with revolts against hunger and unemployment that broke out in 1907. Aimed both at ʿAbd al-ʿAzīz and the Europeans, the rebels attacked French landowners around Casablanca and killed a French doctor in Marrakesh. At the same time, dissensions appeared in the Sultan's family as well. His brother, ʿAbd al-Ḥafīẓ, rose in Marrakesh and declared himself Sultan with the aid of some of the major southern *qāʾid* families, led by Madanī al-Glāwī.[17] In the north, another dissident, the Sufi leader Muḥammad al-Kattānī, had for some time agitated for moral conservatism and against reforms inspired by foreigners. Now, the religious scholars of Fez, who had always been influential in the choice of Sultan, joined him, and gave their endorsement to ʿAbd al-Ḥafīẓ. Having thus support from both the north and the south of the country, he could then move on ʿAbd al-ʿAzīz. The French backed ʿAbd al-ʿAzīz and sent soldiers across the border from Algeria. They also bombarded Casablanca on the coast, and occupied the area around the town. However, the internal revolt was only strengthened by this foreign interference and spread across the country, and in the end ʿAbd al-ʿAzīz was forced to abdicate from the throne in 1908.

ʿAbd al-Ḥafīẓ was thus in power, but he found himself in the same situation as his brother had been: he could no more turn the economy around and repay the creditors than ʿAbd al-ʿAzīz had done, and so the foreigners' stranglehold remained. Morocco was in reality already governed by Europeans. As a result, his former ally al-Kattānī turned against him, and was, as a consequence, murdered on the Sultan's orders. But more revolts arose, now against him, and he was unable to suppress them. So, the French put an end to the situation, and in 1912 sent an army across from Algeria to take direct control of Morocco.

ʿAbd al-Ḥafīẓ was forced to resign, but the French did not want to make Morocco a colony.[18] The French General Lyautey instead imposed another of the Sultan's brothers, Yūsuf, on the throne, and only took the title of 'Resident' (*résident-général*) for himself. Thus, Morocco became a protectorate, formally independent, but governed and administrated by French civil servants; they made the laws, they decided the policies. The Sultan was to become no more than a formal figure with no actual influence.

The French invasion did not quell all the revolts, but managed to contain them to the desert-edge regions in the far south.[19] Many of the *qāʾids* found it beneficial to cooperate with the new rulers, and the last pockets of militant opposition were suppressed. By the early 1930s, the French had full control over Morocco. Or rather, over the part of Morocco that was their protectorate. Spain had finally made a move to push forward their interests too, in the wake of the French advance. They took charge of a strip of land along the Mediterranean coast, with Tetuan as its largest town. In this fairly small region, they set up their own protectorate on the French model. In theory, these Spanish territories were also under the suzerainty of the same Sultan in Rabat,[20] so Morocco was still seen as one country, but divided between two European protectors.

From reform to protectorate in Tunisia

Tunisia's history in the nineteenth century displays many similarities to that of Morocco. Both had rulers who saw the need for reforms to restore imbalances in the economy and society. Both saw the military as the most important area for reform and put their greatest efforts there, in order to strengthen the ruler's power and preserve the country's independence. But the reforms were, in both cases, half-hearted or temporary, and turned out instead to provide an avenue for Europeans to influence and control the country by economic power before they intervened militarily.

The Bey of Tunis had one additional problem that the Moroccan ruler did not share: he was formally subject to the Ottoman Sultan. This had not had any practical effect for centuries, but when the sultan took direct control of the province of Tripolitania next door in 1835, the Bey started to worry that this might be the beginning of a more extensive drive. He thus welcomed the increased French presence in Algeria, since he saw this as a counterbalance to the more dangerous Ottoman threat. At the same time, he made sure to placate the Sultan as much as was convenient, and congratulated him on the change of power in Tripoli. But when the young Bey Aḥmad came to power in 1837, he politely declined the invitation from Istanbul to pay a formal tribute to the Sultan. That would be a step too far in recognizing Ottoman supremacy.

Aḥmad Bey resumed the process of modernization that had been left dormant after Ḥammūda's death twenty years earlier.[21] He did not technically apply the Ottoman *tanẓimāt* reforms, as Tunisia was to find its own way, but the reforms he did introduce were fairly similar to the Ottoman model. He spent large sums in developing his own *niẓāmī* army and brought in French officers to train his new troops. He found an occasion to test their efficiency in the Crimean war in 1855. Aḥmad Bey offered the Ottomans his support, not as an underling but as a fellow ruler, and sent his best troops to the front in Russia. However, it never really came to the test, as the army was so reduced by illness on the journey to Crimea that it never actually saw battle.

Aḥmad initiated a number of other reform programmes, but most of his resources were used on the army. His ambition was to turn Tunisia into a power comparable to those of Europe, but he spent much more on this dream than the country could afford. He thus took up enormous loans from European creditors, piling up a mountain of debts that became the core of Tunisia's problems for the rest of the century.

In the same way as after Ḥammūda's death, the reformist Bey was followed by others who let the reforms slide. Aḥmad Bey had died just before the Crimean debacle, and his successor Muḥammad (1855–1859) stopped most of the reform programmes. Instead he tried to finance Tunisia's debt repayment by raising the taxation level, but turned the screws so far that it damaged the agriculture, and his rule was considered harsh. It sparked an opposition that demanded both an ease of taxation and political reform. The European powers supported these demands, since they needed the Tunisian economy to have sufficient productivity to pay off the debts they were owed. Thus, the Bey had to accept a reform programme that, among other points, gave civil rights to all citizens irrespective of religion (the *ʿahd al-amān*, 1857).

His brother Muḥammad Ṣādiq, who succeeded him in 1859, was pressed to carry out further reforms, including enacting a constitution for Tunisia in 1861. This was the first constitution ever implemented in any Middle Eastern country. It introduced a council that should have the right even to depose the Bey, at least in theory. State and religion were separated, and a new secular penal code was to be formulated. However, this liberal period was to be brief. Even though most of these ideas followed European patterns, and the constitution had actually been formulated under European pressure, the Europeans changed their minds. The political reforms were not accompanied by a change in economic policy; on the contrary, taxes were almost doubled by the Prime Minister, the very powerful Muḥammad Khaznadār. Spontaneous riots broke out, and the French feared that these would lead to the fall of the Bey. Under the constitution, this event would give all power to Khaznadār, whom the French considered to be too pro-British. They therefore made the Bey rescind the constitution after only three years.

Thus, there were two factors that decided Tunisia's policies in this period.[22] One was local rivalry and political dissent within the local elite, with Muḥammad Ṣādiq Bey as a more or less disinterested onlooker; the other was the changing interests of the European creditors and the rivalry between them, in particular between France and England. This influenced both Tunisian internal and external politics. The French saw Istanbul as an ally to England, and therefore supported those forces or persons in Tunis that they felt kept the furthest distance from the Sultan.

Most important, however, were the economic problems and the state's finances. Tunisia was constantly on the brink of ruin, unable to service its debts, and ever harsher new conditions were imposed for extending its credit. Thus, the national debt only grew larger. The foreign creditors had contradictory interests in this. On the one hand, they wanted their loans to be repaid as far as possible and as quickly as possible. On the other, if they squeezed the Tunisian debtors so much that the economy collapsed completely, they would receive nothing. Thus, they supported reforms that could at least partially get Tunisia back on its feet.

This led to an historical drama that has one clear villain and one shining hero, who were, as it happens, closely related by marriage. The villain of the piece was the Prime Minister, Muhammad Khaznadār, a *mamlūk* of Turkish origin who was in the Bey's inner circle and had an extensive network in the country's elite. He worked hard to achieve his primary aim: to garner as much wealth as possible for himself and for his cronies. That meant not only that he was corrupt—a feature shared no doubt by many leading politicians of his time—but he seemed to surpass the general greed by pursuing a policy that consciously and with determination drove Tunisia into ruin, lining his own pockets in the process. Instead of negotiating repayment deals that would improve Tunisia's chances of getting out of its predicament, he instead pressed for agreements with completely impossible conditions, because he received a percentage of the amount involved; so the higher the amounts to be paid, the more he and those he favoured gained.

The hero was Khaznadār's son-in-law, Khayr al-Dīn Pāshā. Also a *mamlūk* of the same background as his nemesis, he first came to notice as the member of a crisis commission that the French had imposed on the country.[23] This came about at the insistence of Napoléon III, because the Tunisian crisis had started to hurt French petty investors, who formed an important part of the French emperor's political base. Thus, it was becoming more imperative for the government in Paris to make sure that something was done in Tunisia. They demanded that a reform commission be set up with one French and one Tunisian member, the latter then being Khayr al-Dīn. The commission proposed an extensive programme, the most important point being that the Tunisian Prime Minister should no longer have the monopoly on renegotiations of loan agreements. This evidently made Khaznadār into Khayr al-Dīn's bitter enemy, but France put its weight behind the proposal and the Bey was forced to fire Khaznadār and appoint Khayr al-Dīn as Prime Minister in 1873.

In his new position, Khayr al-Dīn began a broad series of ambitious reforms that went far beyond the finance sector. He had developed his plan in the book *Aqwam al-masālik* from 1869. While he was not able to realize all of his programme, he did initiate an education reform that was to become perhaps the most important of his efforts. He introduced new subjects into the traditional Zaytūna university, but primarily established a new school called the Ṣādiqī school, named after the Bey. This was to educate many of Tunisia's new leaders in the following century. He also reformed local administration and reorganized the economically important properties of the *waqf* religious foundations. He favoured industrialization, but this was an impossible prospect given the country's precarious finances. Instead, he eased the tax burden on agriculture to improve production in this sector, and also promoted the development of local manufacture.

All this was along lines that the French backers would approve. They were less happy that Khayr al-Dīn also wanted to modernize the legal structure of Tunisia, and in particular the rules that accorded foreign nationals special privileges. He abolished the 'mixed courts' that had settled disputes between Tunisians and foreigners, and where the foreign consuls, not the Tunisian state, had been the determining force. He instead wanted to have a unified and modernized law in common for Tunisians and foreigners. This was not good from a French viewpoint. Nor did they like his efforts to increase Tunisia's freedom to manoeuvre in foreign policy. They suspected that he was working for a rapprochement with the sultan in Istanbul and thus, in their eyes, inching closer to the British. How far Khayr al-Dīn actually went in this direction is not clear, but it seems evident that he was trying to draw on improved relations with Istanbul to achieve greater balance in Tunisia's foreign policies, that is, to reduce its subservience to France.

This was not in Paris's interest, and they decided that Khayr al-Dīn had become an encumbrance. He did of course still have many enemies among those whose interests he had crossed, and the Bey was only too happy to depose Khayr al-Dīn from his post in 1877, after only four years in power.

So, things returned to the way they had been. But this did not, of course, solve Tunisia's underlying financial problems, and Paris could not just let things slide; the reforms were necessary. But since local reforms could apparently work against French interests as well as working for them, it was better that the French did the job themselves. So they began preparations for taking control. In 1881, a local squabble between two tribes on the border with Algeria provided the necessary excuse, and a French detachment crossed the border from Algeria, marched on the capital without meeting any resistance, and presented their demands to the Bey. As he did not have the military strength to oppose them, the Bey had thus to sign the treaty dictated by the French, which became known as the 'Bardo Agreement' after the name of the Bey's palace where it was signed.

The French system of rule was thus a protectorate. The Bey remained the 'ruler' of Tunsia, under the formal overlordship of the Ottoman Sultan (who was of course in no way consulted). Neither of the two were however to have any real power in the country. As in Morocco a generation later, the French ruled through a *résident*, and the government was composed of French administrators. Only the Prime Minister and one other minister were Tunisian, neither of the two with any real influence on policy. The government was not directed by the Prime Minister, but by the Resident alone.

4

THE PROTECTORATES AND NATIONALISM

The French had already been ruling Algeria for 50 years when they entered their new territory of Tunisia. Thus, they had an established model for how to govern a Maghrebi country. But one thing the new French masters of Tunisia were certain of was that they should avoid that model. They saw the Algerian experience as a series of mistakes and fumbles that had to be avoided at all costs. And the most serious mistake was to give the European colonists the power and influence that they had in Algeria.

In Algeria, the idea had been to construct a new, European society without regard for the existing inhabitants, their culture and social structures. In the protectorates, the Europeans instead worked within these structures, albeit on their own terms and with their own ends in mind. Thus, the French who came to Tunisia found Khayr al-Dīn's reform programme very useful and, at least in its basic principles, a way forward out of the crisis. They just did not think that the Tunisians were capable of carrying it out. The French had to do it themselves. Thus, they continued implementing the administrative reforms that Khayr al-Dīn had started, and brought in French technicians, specialists in agricultural development and in other fields, who helped make these sectors, and eventually also an industrial sector, grow.

Some land was transferred to European ownership in Tunisia and Morocco, as had been done in Algeria. But the transfers were on a much smaller scale in the two protectorates, and the settlers who got this land were also kept further away from a decisive influence, something that often angered them. They did have strong opinions, and were very often critical of reforms that favoured the Arab inhabitants, following the example of their fellows in Algeria. On occasion, they could also find a sympathetic ear with a resident if he was at odds with any liberal proposal from Paris, but they were not able to force their politics on the authorities. So, while they never got the independent power they had in Algeria, the *colons* of Tunisia and Morocco could form alliances with some residents but were ignored by others, according to the politics of the day.

Morocco under European rule

The French maintained Morocco's formal independence as a sultanate throughout the period they ruled the country. They allowed the Sultan to keep both his Prime Minister (*wazīr*) and several other ministers, who were often recruited from major *qāʾid* or other notable families. In addition, the French created a largely parallel administration that took its orders from the Resident.[1] Thus, the Sultan's government was largely powerless and a formality. Sultan Yūsuf accepted the role he was assigned and did not try to influence political developments. However, the Sultan's court did remain a centre for discussion, intrigue and possible political assertions, with its own interests.

The broad lines of French rule were laid out by the first Resident, General Lyautey. His primary goals were to consolidate French military control over Morocco and to stabilize the country. He continued the Sultan's policy of ruling through local notables, *qāʾid*s, since these were better able to harness control over their respective territories and prevent any resistance to the growth of the new rulers. He strengthened the power of the chosen *qāʾid*s by merging several regions, so that fewer and more powerful families controlled larger territories. The family that perhaps gained most from these changes was the most powerful of them all, the Glāwīs from the Marrakesh region. Their leader, Madanī al-Glāwī, had helped put the rebel Sultan ʿAbd al-Ḥafīẓ on the throne in 1909, and had lost his post as *wazīr* when the French ousted that Sultan. However, he quickly turned around to become Lyautey's ally and was soon one of the richest men in Morocco. When he died in 1918, his brother Thāmī al-Glāwī inherited his position and rose to become the dominant landowner in southern Morocco. He later also became a successful industrialist.

Lyautey supported agricultural reforms, which were primarily to the advantage of the French, but could in some circumstances also benefit the Moroccans. French landowners took control over considerable areas of agricultural land, where they introduced commercial farming, merging smaller units into large. Such intensified exploitation required more water, so extensive irrigation projects were also launched. These developments divided Moroccan farmers. Many of them were forced off the land and moved to the towns to seek work. Other farmers were able to benefit from the irrigation projects, and the largest landowners began to follow the example of the French and establish larger commercial holdings. This increased their profits, and the Glāwīs and other similar prosperous families began to gain fortunes that could compare to those of the French. However, the majority of the rural population were worse off after these changes.

Even though the anti-colonial resistance was able to survive for some 20 years on the desert-edge in the far south, it never put the new rulers in any serious danger. It was rather the north that saw the most significant anti-European rebellion, and it was directed at the Spanish, not the French protectors. One of the most important *qāʾid*s in the narrow stretch administered by Spain was Aḥmad al-Raysūnī. He had been among the notables who supported ʿAbd al-Ḥafīẓ in 1909, and he soon ran foul of the Spanish when they tried to undermine his authority. He called for a *jihād* against them, and the Spanish were unable to stop his raids.

However, the revolt became rather more serious when it was taken over by a younger and better educated reformist leader in 1919. Muḥammad ibn ʿAbd al-Karīm al-Khaṭṭābī, known to the Europeans as Abdel-Krim, made his recruitments far beyond the narrow circle of tribal leaders that al-Raysūnī had appealed to.[2] Abdel-Krim organized a fairly modern rebel army in the northern area known as the Rif, and his revolt is thus known as the 'Rif War'. He conquered several Spanish posts and hurt both the Spanish army and its prestige. He declared a 'Rif Republic', which was hardly a republic, but rather a traditional rebel stronghold that was able to keep the Spanish at bay for several years. But in 1925 he made the mistake of crossing the demarcation line into French-held territory and marched on Fez. In spite of its successes against the Spanish, his army was no match for the superior French forces, and together, the two European powers drove Abdel-Krim's republic into submission the following year.

Abdel-Krim's movement must basically be seen as a continuation of the early resistance against colonial expansion, but it also contained elements that pointed forward to another age. He was himself a supporter of the Salafi movement. The term *salafi* has been applied to a variety of different trends in Islam that in various ways used the early community of believers, the *salaf*, as a model. Today, Saudi Arabia as well as radical Islamists are often called Salafis. However, the term was used differently in early twentieth-century Maghreb. It was an extension of the teachings of the reformer Muḥammad ʿAbduh in Egypt (d. 1905), who had worked for a 'purified' and rational Islam suitable to modern society.[3] Abduh modernized education and introduced natural sciences alongside religious knowledge in Muslim schools. His followers in the Maghreb focused particularly on this educational aspect of his reform, so Salafism here was primarily a movement for educational reform and for opening up religious education to modern sciences. The most famous figure was ʿAbd al-Ḥamīd Ben Bādīs from Algeria, and Abdel-Krim supported his efforts.

This was also the view of those who were to lay the foundations for a modern nationalist movement in Morocco.[4] One of them was ʿAllāl al-Fāsī, who had received a traditional education at the Qarawīyīn university in Fez and had encountered reformist ideas there. He and a number of other scholars established a series of 'free schools' at the beginning of the 1920s, which, according to the Salafi ideal, combined reformist Islam with western science, but were independent of the colonial authorities. These schools filled an obvious need as the French did little to support education for Muslim Moroccans. Several graduates from these free schools went on to further education in France and returned with radical ideas about self-rule. Towards the end of the 1920s the first strands of what we may call an incipient Moroccan nationalism began to coalesce.

There were also other sources for Moroccan nationalism. Urbanization and economic hardship had caused many Moroccans to leave the country for France in search of work, in particular after World War I. Many of them joined trade unions that, at this time, were radicalized. Workers from all countries of the Maghreb formed a separate union of their own, the *Étoile Nord-Africaine*, which was close to the communists. Some of its members returned to Morocco in the late 1920s and began to organize urban workers there. Their focus was economic, working for improved workers' rights, but they also had nationalist overtones.

These new trends were thus stronger in the cities than in the countryside. Clubs, unions and associations were formed to work for Morocco's interests. They did not yet demand independence, but that Moroccans should have more say in the protectorate's affairs. They wanted its government to be a real partnership between Moroccans and France, rather than a purely French affair.

The Resident did not, however, respond favourably to these suggestions.[5] Lyautey had been replaced after the Abdel-Krim conflict and his successors were conservatives who did not approve of greater Arab–Muslim participation. Instead, they focused on Morocco's Berber minority, which they wanted to favour over the 'more Islamic' Arabs. They proposed a separate regulation (*dāhir*) for the Berbers, by which these were to be ruled according to their 'customary laws' rather than the regular, and partially Sharīʿa-based, Moroccan state laws. The *dāhir*, which was passed in 1930, also gave the Berbers internal autonomy within Morocco. The new regulation led to great protests from the nationalists who correctly saw it as an attempt to divide and conquer. This became the first important cause around which the nationalists could rally support, and it caused a considerable stir as far as the nationalist circles in the Mashreq.

Sultan Yūsuf had died in 1927, so it fell to his son, Muḥammad V, to sign the *dāhir*. Just like his father, the young Sultan always stuck to the protectorate agreement and never openly challenged the French authorities. But he clearly favoured a stronger role for the Moroccans in the partnership, and his sympathy for the nationalist cause was no secret. He allowed himself to be entitled *malik*, King, from 1934, but to the French he was never more than a Sultan. Thus, in spite of his enforced passivity in his relations to the French, he became a focus for nationalist sentiment, even though he also retained excellent relations with the traditional *qāʾid* families such as the Glāwīs, who were not close to the nationalist circles.

There were several large strikes in the 1930s, in particular in 1936, when France elected a radical Popular Front government, giving hope to the nationalist cause. But there were also internal conflicts and rivalries among the nationalists, and several competing parties were formed. When a large demonstration in 1937 resulted in clashes in which thirteen people died, the Resident banned the nationalist parties. ʿAllāl al-Fāsī, the most prominent nationalist leader, was exiled to Gabon.

The nationalists found an ally in the Spanish authorities in their northern strip.[6] While these followed France's example in how to run their protectorate, they were also rivals and looked with considerable sympathy on the Moroccan nationalists, as long as they aimed their campaigns against France. However, the

Spanish zone of Morocco was to become more famous for a different event: it was from here that General Franco began his rebellion against the Spanish republic in 1936. The Left in Spain saw the area as a den of reaction, and had, in general, little interest in Moroccan affairs.

However, events in Europe were to play a larger role in the history of the Maghreb after France fell to German forces in 1940. Resident Nougès had been appointed by the left-wing government, but chose to follow Vichy. Nevertheless, he used Morocco's formal independence as an excuse to limit German influence. The Sultan was also very cautious, and refused to implement Germany's demands for a Jewish policy, a line that served him well after the war. But Jewish refugees were still gathered in camps in the Sahara during the Vichy period, and Jews also suffered from various restrictions in employment and domicile.

The pro-German government, however, lasted only two and a half years as allied forces under US command landed in Morocco in November 1942. Many of the French there sympathized with de Gaulle's Free French forces, and offered only token resistance. The presence of the Americans had a great impact on Morocco, not least because of their outspoken anti-colonial views. Still, the pre-war system of a protectorate was reintroduced, as de Gaulle had no intention of dismantling the French empire. But many Moroccans pointed out that the legitimacy for France's role as 'protector' was that it should protect Morocco, and the French had clearly shown that they were not able to do this in 1940. Thus, the basis for protectorate rule was no longer there.

Unrest grew over the next few years. The main nationalist groups merged in 1944 to form the *Isitqlāl* ('Independence') party, and when ʿAllāl al-Fāsī returned from exile in 1946, he became the uncontested leader of the party. There were also more radical tendencies within Istiqlāl, such as the trade unionist and socialist Mehdī Ben Barka. In spite of his left-wing leanings, Ben Barka was also well received at the Sultan's palace, and became the tutor of the young crown prince, Muḥammad's son

Ḥasan. The nationalists could also benefit from the French–Spanish rivalry, as the latter gave them a safe haven in their zone. However, the Spanish authorities were less happy when the Sultan visited Tangiers in their zone in 1947. He was welcomed as a national hero, and used the occasion to emphasize that Morocco was one unified country and thus a natural candidate for independence.

In Paris, governments of various left- and right-wing combinations alternated in power, and did not carry any consistent policy towards Morocco. Some supported reforms that generally proposed too little too late; others followed a hard-line approach spurred on by the local French settlers. The Resident Guillaume came eventually to follow the latter approach. In addition to the settlers, he allied with the traditional *qāʾid* leaders, who had now become a prosperous upper class that looked with apprehension on the more radical nationalists and feared that the Sultan supported the nationalist cause over their interests. Some of them also had their own quarrels with the palace. ʿAbd al-Ḥayy al-Kattānī, one of the more influential traditional leaders, had never forgiven that Sultan ʿAbd al-Ḥafīẓ had given orders in 1909 for his father to be whipped to death. Together with the great *qāʾid* Thāmī al-Glāwī, he approached the Resident and argued that the Sultan was a key to the problems and had to be removed.

Following this, al-Glāwī called a meeting with some major *qāʾid*s in 1953 and declared the Sultan deposed in favour of a distant cousin. Several other traditional leaders quickly opposed this move, which they said had no constitutional basis, and it led to riots in favour of the Sultan. But the declaration gave Guillaume an excuse to 'accede to their demand' and exile Sultan Muḥammad to Madagascar.

However, this attempt to stave off the inevitable failed. And it was again French defeats in distant wars that provoked the change. The dismal failure of the French colonial army against the Vietnamese nationalists at Dien Bien Phu in the spring of 1954 sparked the violent rebellion in Algeria in the autumn of that year. Thus, France had more pressing matters to attend to than to worry about local intrigues in Morocco. A new left-wing government in Paris decided that it was impossible to continue as before in Morocco, a view that was in part reinforced by increased unrest in the country. Small groups threatening terrorist action were formed both among the settlers and among the most radical nationalists. In 1955, a group that called itself the 'Liberation Army for the Arab Maghreb', composed of Algerians, Moroccans and other Arabs, landed on the coast in the south and attempted to start a guerrilla campaign. This group supported the Sultan/King, but rejected the more moderate Istiqlāl nationalists.

Paris, therefore, invited the nationalists to a conference where they accepted Morocco's independence. The Sultan was reinstated, and even Glāwī now asked for, and received, a pardon from his sovereign, before the old *qā'id* died soon after. The French protectorate came to an end on 2 March 1956, and Morocco became an independent kingdom. General Franco was quite unhappy with these events, but it was impossible for Spain to maintain a protectorate when the French had abolished theirs. Thus, the Spanish also withdrew on 7 April, except for the old enclaves of Ceuta and Melilla on the Mediterranean coast, and Sidi Ifni in the south; the latter territory was restored to Morocco in 1969.

Tunisia: Destour nationalism

The developments in Morocco and Tunisia were in many ways parallel, but there were also distinctions, in part because of their different histories.[7] The clearest difference was the role that the Sultan had played in Morocco. While he always stayed within the boundaries that the protectorate masters had set up for his position, he still came to be a national symbol and an important element in the struggle for independence.

The Bey in Tunis had just as much—or as little—power in his country as the Moroccan had in his, under French rule. But, with one or two exceptions, he did not play any role in the nationalist campaign. He became irrelevant almost immediately after the French had taken power, and disappeared from the country's political history.

As we have seen, the traditional nobility, the *qāʾid*s, played a significant part in the Moroccan economy and as a conservative force in politics. Tunisia also had its own *qāʾid* system of local notables. But these did not have the same influence as the large tribal leaders in Morocco. The authority of the Tunisian *qāʾid*s was soon undermined by the French. While the Moroccans moved towards fewer and larger *qāʾid* areas, the French in Tunisia split their administration into many more and smaller entities, giving each of them less clout both locally and in national politics. The French also imposed 'controllers' to supervise the activities of the *qāʾid*s and thus integrated them into their own administration, rather than leaving them as independent actors as in Morocco.

But, again as in Morocco, the French rule in Tunisia was not a complete break with the social system they had found. In many ways, they took over the existing state structures, thus continuing Khayr al-Dīn's reform programme. However, they put French personnel into that system. The government was filled with French administrators (except for the *wazīr* and 'secretary', neither with any real power). The Resident became Minister for Foreign Affairs, and the Bey no longer controlled the army. The military was reformed and modernized under French command, and state bureaucracy grew. Tunisians were still employed in the administration, but only in subaltern positions. The higher levels were reserved for French officials, who occupied about two-thirds of the posts in the administration, the rest being left to Tunisians, whose wages were also only two-thirds those of a Frenchman in the same position.

As the general idea was that only the French could run Tunisia competently, little effort was put into educating Tunisians. Khayr al-Dīn's Ṣādiqī school was allowed to continue its activity, but did not have the capacity to answer the demand for education. Some missionary and other 'French–Arab' schools were opened, but only a few Tunisians were allowed to enrol there.

Thus, most Tunisians still went to the traditional religious *kuttāb* schools. The highest level of this classical Islamic school system was the Zaytūna university, which had a long tradition of learning, but focused only on the classical religious disciplines. There were reformist tendencies also among the Zaytūna scholars, but they were in a minority. The classical *ʿulamāʾ* scholars disapproved of the suggestions to change the system.[8]

Instead, these religious reformists began constructing a parallel school system called the Khaldūnīya schools, named after the great medieval philosopher and scientist Ibn Khaldūn. These were to be modern schools with a modern curriculum of natural and humanist sciences, and were meant as an addition to the Zaytūna education for the students who went to that university or came directly from the traditional *kuttāb*s. They should thus get both a classical education and a modern one. In this way, the Khaldūnīya schools had a slightly different emphasis from the Ṣādiqī school, which was purely secular, but the two systems complemented each other. Together, they provided a modern education for a new Tunisian elite that was groomed for social reform and, fully competent in French, the language of the colonial master, eager to use their competence for the good of Tunisia. Many also travelled to France for further education and were even more influenced by French culture there.

These educated elites were mostly recruited from the urban middle and upper classes. Most Tunisians still worked on the land. Here, too, the agriculture came under pressure from European settlers. They bought up land, particularly that owned by absentee landlords and cultivated by sharecroppers. For the owners, this was just a property transaction, but the effects were more dire for the peasants when the settlers turned the larger properties into commercial farms that had no room for the sharecroppers. Many of these were forced off the land and moved to the towns, where they provided a pool of available labour. This did not involve all agriculture; there were also independent farmers who continued to cultivate their own land, often more marginal and less productive and thus of less interest to the foreign settlers. The settlers were, incidentally, not necessarily French; there were at times twice as many Italian residents in Tunisia as French, many of them agriculturalists.

Tunisia did, like Morocco, thus always have a functioning 'civil society' with political ambitions, unlike the Algerian situation. As in Morocco, the French in Tunisia vacillated between answering these ambitions by promising reform, and suppressing dissent; depending on the political currents in Paris, the inclination of the Resident and the strength of the settlers, who here as elsewhere argued for a harsh line against the locals.

The development of Tunisian nationalism may be divided into three stages or generations.[9] The first grew out of the reform movements of the Khaldūnīya schools and had its social base in the old class of notables from the pre-colonial period (the 'mamlūks'). They took the name *Jeunes tunisiens*, emulating the 'Young Turks' of Istanbul. This current, which grew around the turn of the century, accepted that Tunisia needed a 'protector', but wanted a greater balance between Tunisians and French in a true partnership. The Resident had set up a 'consultative assembly', and the reformists demanded equal representation of Tunisians and French in this body. The Resident did indeed include some Tunisians into the assembly in 1907, but so few that they had no real influence over its decisions. Tensions between the French and the Tunisian community sharpened in the first decade of the new century, and there were clashes between locals and French (and Italian) settlers in some towns in 1911. As a response, the Young Tunisians' newspapers were banned and their leaders exiled. Subsequently this current faded away.

After World War I, however, new ideas about self-rule began to surface. The war had led to economic development and better fortunes for a rising new Tunisian middle class, and growing radicalism in Europe found an echo in Tunisia. The leaders of the former Young Tunisians movement were allowed to return to Tunisia, and one of these, ʿAbd al-ʿAzīz al-Thaʿālabī, formed a new liberal party in 1920. Its aim was to get a new constitution, *dustūr* in Arabic, and the party thus became known as the 'Destour party'.

Tha'ālabī was himself of the old Zaytūna generation that had dominated the earlier movement, but he progressed from the cautious talk about just influencing the colonial power towards a more radical position. The new party was able to move into new social groups; their strength lay in the new and increasingly prosperous middle class, which felt hemmed in by the French refusal to give Tunisians any responsibility in the administration. The Destour did still talk of 'partnership' with the French, but it should be a real partnership with an independent, and strong, Tunisian voice.

It all mattered little to the authorities. Even if they at times engaged in talks with the nationalists, they basically considered them to be a danger to French interests and the future of the French presence in Tunisia, and had no intention of acceding to their demands. They became seriously concerned when the Destour was able to convince the Bey, Nāṣir Bey, to support their demands in 1922. But the crisis was dissolved when the Bey died soon after and his successor supported the French. The authorities' lack of responsiveness radicalized the Destour, and they began to collect funds for Abdel-Krim's revolt in Morocco. Again, the mood became more tense with an increase in strikes and unrest. But when the Resident clamped down on the protests, the Destour were not able to respond. Following this, they went into decline. The time had come for a third generation of nationalists to take up the mantle and lead the country to independence.

The leader of this new surge was the young lawyer Ḥabīb Bourguiba, who returned to Tunisia in 1927 after having completed his studies in France.[10] He soon become involved in nationalist politics, and travelled around the country to drum up support for the Destour party. However, he soon came to believe that their demands for 'a constitution' were insufficient. Tha'ālabī and the other old leaders of the party did not listen to Bourguiba and the other young radicals, who called for a change in the party's attitudes. Thus, a large group of younger members broke away in 1934 to form a new party. They preserved the link to their political past by retaining the term '*destour*', but this was then the *new* Destour party, *le Parti Néo-Destourien*.

Soon after, Léon Blum's Popular Front government took power in Paris, and allowed the nationalist forces to operate more freely in Tunisia. Bourguiba was thus able to build up his party, until the Blum government fell the following year and the possibilities for political activism were again curtailed.

Thus, there were at this time two competing nationalist movements: Thaʿālabī's 'old' Destour and Bourguiba's Neo-Destour. Although the latter was a left-wing split, the two often competed in radicalism. Thaʿālabī could talk of 'independence' at times when Bourguiba found it more politic to speak only of autonomy, and vice versa. There were certainly elements of personal rivalry and ambition in the conflicts between the two parties; but there were also differences that were more fundamental in nature.

There was certainly a generation gap between them, but also one of social background. The old Destour had its basis primarily in the capital Tunis and one or two of the other largest towns, in a middle class based on land property and trade, but also among upper-level functionaries. The Neo-Destour leaders also came from a fairly affluent middle-class background, but their geographical basis was much wider: Bourguiba himself came from Monastir in the south, a region the urbanites of Tunis found provincial and unappealing.

The younger politicians were also, to a much larger degree, educated by modern schools—Ṣādiqī or Khaldūnīya—than their predecessors. Many of them were fully integrated into French culture: thus Bourguiba had studied in France and had a French wife. They were familiar with Arab culture and referred occasionally to the Islamic heritage, but their generation had been 'modernized' into a francophone mould. This made it even more vexing that the French still considered the Tunisians not sufficiently 'mature' to govern themselves, needing French patrons to do it for them.

The Neo-Destour also innovated in their political methods. The old Destour party claimed a large membership, but mainly acted by writing declarations and petitioning the authorities. Bourguiba instead began to build a mass party and organized large-scale demonstrations in a far more efficient way. The Neo-Destour widened their activities throughout the country rather than focusing only on the capital, and grew roots beyond the middle class from which they originated, gaining support in the countryside and also nurturing contacts with budding workers' organizations that the old Destour rather disdained.

These changes in the political and social landscape did not go unnoticed by the authorities. Many liberal or radical voices among the French suggested reforms. But the government also had to consider the political weight of the settlers, who owned much of the best land and had extensive property interests in Tunisia. Even if they never had as much political clout as those in Algeria, the Tunisian settlers were sufficiently powerful to have an impact on French policy, and particularly so when they could find allies among the right-wing forces in metropolitan politics. Their aim was the same as their Algerian fellows: to stop any reforms, be it to increase Tunisian participation in local government, or give the locals 'dangerous' modern education. The resident was thus torn between reformist proposals and the settlers' resistance to change.

World War II brought a number of changes. The Tunisian resident did as his Moroccan counterpart, and joined the pro-German Vichy government. The nationalist parties were banned. At the same time many nationalists rejoiced that France had been defeated, and the movement was divided into a pro-Allies and a pro-German wing. The Vichy authorities sent Bourguiba to Rome in the hope that he would agitate against de Gaulle's Free French forces from there. But he refused to participate unless Vichy and its allies guaranteed Tunisian independence; something they would not do.

In this turmoil, a new voice made itself heard. The Bey had—apart from the short episode in 1922—been completely irrelevant to Tunisian politics ever since he signed the Bardo agreement in 1881. Now, however, a new incumbent, Moncef Bey, who had acceded to the throne in 1942 and had nationalist sympathies, tried to make a move. He never voiced direct support for the Axis powers, remaining formally neutral, but he was allowed greater influence over local affairs than his predecessors. He used the occasion to appoint a new all-Tunisian government. It was composed partly of members from (old) Destour, the trend with which Moncef was most comfortable, but the prime ministership was given to Muḥammad Chenik, a businessman who was close to Bourguiba.

However, Moncef Bey's Tunisian government did not last long: the allied invasion came only a year later; Moncef Bey was considered a collaborator and was deposed in favour of his cousin, Amīn Bey. Many of the nationalists who had worked with Moncef were arrested. Although the Neo-Destour had not formally joined his government and Bourguiba had publicly condemned any collaboration with the Vichy authorities, that party was also banned and the Resident took direct control over the protectorate.

At the time, de Gaulle had made some remarks about the possibility for future Tunisian self-rule, but liberated France did nothing to pursue this suggestion. The nationalists were weakened by events during the war, and Bourguiba decided in 1945 to go into self-imposed exile in Cairo to try to gain international support for his cause. He left the task of rebuilding the Neo-Destour under the ban to the party secretary, Ṣālaḥ ben Yūsuf.

The Neo-Destour were not the only force among the nationalists. Many, particularly on the more moderate or conservative wing, still saw Moncef Bey as the best solution for Tunisian autonomy, and formed a committee to have him returned to the position of Bey. This became a rallying cry for the 'old' Destour after their historical leader Thaʿālabī died in 1944, but also for religious traditionalists who looked with disfavour on the 'modernists' of the Neo-Destour. A popular sentiment did indeed develop in favour of this demand, but the Resident was quite unwilling to allow this nationalist figurehead back on the throne. The Moncef campaign abated when Moncef Bey died in 1948, and the old Destour party also largely disappeared from the forefront of politics, together with the Moncef campaign.

Another force was to become much more important in this difficult period for Tunisian nationalism. The Tunisians who had moved from the countryside to the towns joined a growing working class. The first attempts in 1920 to organize these workers into a national trade union had failed, but in 1946 the *Union Générale des Travailleurs Tunisiens* (UGTT) was established. It was not the first trade union in Tunisia: a communist affiliate already existed, so the UGTT, which had strong nationalist leanings, was denied membership in the communist world federation (WFTU). Instead, they attached themselves politically to the Neo-Destour. When their first leader, Farḥāt Ḥashād, was murdered by a terrorist group in 1952, leadership fell to the young Aḥmad ben Ṣālaḥ, who was to become one of Tunisia's leading politicians through the 1950s and 1960s.

Bourguiba returned to Tunisia in 1949 and took the reins back from Ben Yūsuf, who had continued rebuilding the party.[11] But the Resident again came down hard on the party after a political crisis in 1952. Bourguiba was put in prison and Ben Yūsuf had to flee. The UGTT, on the other hand, was a legitimate mass organization and was in this period the force that kept the nationalist struggle alive and mobilized opinion for their demands. The steadfast French refusal of any type of reform began to cause anger among increasingly large sections of the population. The authorities began to lose control over parts of the countryside, particularly in the south, which slid towards anarchy. Groups called *fallāgha* began to take control over some regions, some with nationalist aims, others clearly of a more criminal bent. These were spontaneous and local developments, but the nationalists in the Neo-Destour and UGTT made contact with these groups and gave them support. The authorities sent the army to quell the protests, but were not able to regain control.

The French faced many crises in their colonies in 1954, and could not afford to have Tunisia break down as well. A new left-wing government under Pierre Mendez-France therefore approached Bourguiba alongside similar talks taking place in Morocco. The Tunisians agreed to a programme for autonomy in return for making the *fallāgha* lay down their arms, which Bourguiba was able to organize when he was released from prison in 1955. Shortly after, he learned that Paris had promised full independence to Morocco, and demanded the same for Tunisia. The French accepted this, and Tunisia became a fully independent state in March 1956, with Bourguiba as its Prime Minister. A referendum the following year made Tunisia into a republic, ending the reign of the Ḥusaynid beys who had been on the throne since 1705. Bourguiba took over both as President and Prime Minister of the new republic.

5

ARMED RESISTANCE

The imposition of the protectorate had been a fairly peaceful affair both in Morocco and Tunisia, although there had been some revolts in marginal areas: brief in Tunisia, slightly more protracted in Morocco. The nationalist movements had emerged in a modernized middle class that felt hemmed in by French rule, and had been able to grow, mobilize and finally negotiate a peaceful transition to independence under the French. There were in both countries moments of violence and terrorism from extreme groups among the European settlers as well as the nationalists, and threats and fear of more unrest certainly prompted the French willingness to pull out of the protectorates before it was too late. On the whole, however, we must consider the abolition of European rule in those two countries as fairly peaceful transactions, compared to what happened in many other cases.

A major reason for this is clearly the nature of the European system there. A protectorate gave some space for a local middle and upper class, even if they were kept away from political power and were considered inferior to the Europeans. The old upper classes were able to maintain many of their social privileges both in Morocco and in Tunisia, partly by adapting to the new conditions and cooperating with the new masters, partly by changing the nature of their power base from family and clan alone to a more extensive patron-client relationship that involved new social groups. Thus, we can see in both countries that the nascent nationalism had its roots in the reform-oriented elements of the former upper class, but that it gradually changed its social base towards the newly formed middle and working classes.

In the two Maghreb countries where European rule was far more direct, Algeria and Libya, the development was dramatically different. There, there was no gradual transition from old to new politics, but a total rupture in the form of war and revolution in a manner quite opposite to the two neighbours. The contrast between the two groups of countries is also clear in the period after independence, when Morocco and Tunisia have enjoyed largely stable, albeit undemocratic, rule, while Algeria and Libya have been through dramatic and extremely violent convolutions.

There were, however, also important distinctions between the latter two countries. Libya was dominated by a traditional socio-religious system, and it was only in 1969 that the country developed a political system that was not (at least initially) based on tribal distribution and religious authority. In Algeria, on the other hand, we saw that the French had already destroyed the basis of traditional society by the end of the nineteenth century. The nationalist trends grew there in a modernized sector that did not have continuity back to its traditional society as had all the other three countries. It also developed under much harsher conditions, where the absence of a domestic bourgeoisie was important: the only people with money and resources were the French colonialists.

Libya: resistance to the Italians

Italy had always considered Tunisia as a natural part of its sphere of interest. It was the European country that was nearest to Tunisia: less than 100 miles (150 km) across the sea from Sicily, and many fishermen regularly made the journey, some even owning houses on the other side. As noted above, there were two Italians for each French settler in Tunisia. Thus, it was with great reluctance that Rome had to accept that France had beaten them to the establishment of a protectorate. Instead, they began to prepare the great powers for the idea that Italy should at least be allowed to take the last unclaimed parts of the North African shore, Tripolitania and Cyrenaica.

It was only well into the new century, however, as the Ottoman Empire fell into dire crisis, that they began to make their colonial dreams a reality.[1] They declared their intention to occupy 'Libya', as they now baptized the country, and sent forces into Tripolitania as well as Cyrenaica in October 1911. The Ottomans resisted, but did not have many troops on the ground, and when the Balkan wars broke out only a few months later, they gave up. They reluctantly accepted a treaty that the Sultan should be only the religious head of the country, while the Italians should have the political power. However, some Ottoman soldiers were surreptitiously left behind to keep up the resistance.

The Italians at first only settled in some of the towns on the coast. The interior was left without any structured government, and different regions reacted in different ways. A member of the small Berber minority in north-western Tripolitania, Sulaymān al-Bārūnī, raised a resistance force there. He was an experienced politician and had represented Tripolitania in the Ottoman parliament as a dedicated follower of the Young Turk movement, which at this point was in power in Istanbul. From this connection, he was able to gain the support of some Ottoman politicians, in particular Enver Pasha, the later dominant politician, who went to Tripolitania and fought in the resistance. However, Bārūnī's efforts in Tripolitania ended in defeat in 1913.

The centre of resistance came instead to be the poor and marginalized province of Cyrenaica. Its organizer was even more surprising.[2] The Sanūsī Sufi brotherhood had established itself in Cyrenaica in 1841, around its founder Muḥammad ibn ʿAlī al-Sanūsī (d. 1859), a scholar originally from Mustaghanim in Algeria. He began building lodges along the desert edge and in oases in the desert, seeking out Bedouin tribes that were Muslim, but not particularly ardent in their faith. The brotherhood quickly gained support among the rival Bedouin tribes, and became a force of cohesion and unity, without ever seeking to usurp the political independence of each tribal shaykh. By the end of the century, it had between 50 and 100 lodges from Tripolitania in the west to the Egyptian desert in the east, and through the Sahara to Chad in the south. Their aim was to promote religious piety and knowledge among the Bedouin, but they also promoted oasis agriculture and trans-Saharan trade, and helped secure a trade route to the south that became important and profitable at the end of the century. The political implication of this was that, in order to promote this economic development, the various Bedouin groups had to put aside their internal rivalries and fighting and look to the Sufi order that they all related to as a common point of identity.

The brotherhood had no political ambitions, but French scouts in Africa, who had never met the order, had been told they were anti-European fanatics.[3] Thus, when French forces first came across a Sanūsī outpost north of Lake Chad in 1902, they attacked and burned it down. Because of this, the local tribes rallied under the cry of defending 'their' brotherhood and, in spite of itself, it came to be seen as a force of resistance, although the fighting was done by local Saharan tribes. Now, ten years later, the Bedouins remembered these heroic efforts, and as the foreigners had now attacked the Sanūsī heartland of Cyrenaica, they approached the brotherhood's young leader, Aḥmad al-Sharīf, and asked him to organize a resistance movement.

He hesitated and his elders urged him to refuse, as the order was not a militant or military one. But in the end al-Sharīf decided to accept the challenge under the obligation of defensive *jihād* and began to organize the nomadic tribes.[4] He was advised in this by Ottoman officers, who helped train the Bedouins. The tribes joined in considerable numbers, but never came to fight in a classical set fashion; their combat was and remained tribal guerrilla warfare. However, they accepted Sanūsī leadership, and the brotherhood's local shaykhs were transformed into leaders of guerrilla bands. The order also provided central leadership, communications and coordination, which in sum was enough to stop any Italian attempt to move out of their bases on the coast.

The Sanūsīs were thus fairly quickly able to control all the Cyrenaican hinterland. In 1913 the Italians moved into Fezzan, the south-western corner of the new Libyan entity, and occupied the largest oases. However, they were forced out by stiff resistance as soon as the following year. Fighting also broke out again in Tripolitania, now under the tribal leader Ramaḍān al-Suwayḥilī, who established the 'Republic of Tripolitania'. Thus by 1915, Italian control was mostly restricted to a few towns on the coast.[5]

By this time World War I had started, and Italy was an ally of the Entente. The central powers, including Germany and the Ottoman Empire, accordingly supported the anti-Italian resistance. However, their advice was not always very helpful. Enver Pasha, now one of the most prominent Ottoman war leaders, convinced Aḥmad al-Sharīf to take his forces into Egypt and attack the British from there, with the help of Egyptian Bedouins who had good relations with the Sanūsīs and the Cyrenaican tribes. The British and their allies had so far paid little heed to Italy's problems in Libya, the Italian expansion being after all in part due to rivalry with France. But a direct attack from the Sanūsī forces changed matters, and the British were easily able to defeat the Sanūsī incursion. This turned into a catastrophe for al-Sharīf, who was forced to resign from the leadership of the brotherhood under British pressure. Instead, his cousin Muḥammad Idrīs took charge of the brotherhood.

Idrīs had good connections to the British, and was able to sort out the diplomatic rifts fairly quickly.[6] The British were not committed to the Italian ambitions, and clearly saw that Italy had over-extended itself and could not hope to control Libya. Thus, they negotiated a treaty between Italy and the Sanūsīs, the

Acroma agreement of 1917. It gave Idrīs de facto control over eastern Libya, and he could rule there in relative peace in the years that followed.

Suwayḥilī's Tripolitanian republic did not fare so well, in particular after Suwayḥilī was killed in battle in 1920. Combats continued in that region, and the Italians began a more protracted offensive in 1922. When Mussolini took power in Rome later that year, he also intensified the Italian war effort. The Fascists scrapped the Acroma agreement and set about a campaign of conquest that was to last nine years. They were quickly able to subdue Tripolitania, so most of the fighting took place in the east and south of the country.

Idrīs now left Libya for Egypt and led the brotherhood from exile. The tactical leadership of the war was left to local Sanūsī commanders, of whom the most famous was ʻUmar al-Mukhtār.[7] The tribal guerrilla bands could use their knowledge of the terrain to tie down a much larger Italian force. But eventually the Italian superiority in numbers began to wear down the guerrillas. The Italian General Graziani was credited with effecting the final breakthrough, not least because of his ruthlessness; he executed more than 10,000 tribesmen. Particularly effective was his decision in 1930 to collect most of the tribes of northern Cyrenaica into concentration camps, thus cutting off the support that the guerrillas received from their relatives. In the following year the Sanūsī capital of Kufra in the south-eastern desert was captured and sacked. Finally, Mukhtār was captured at the end of 1931 and hanged. With his death, the resistance collapsed, and the Italians could finally turn their attention to fulfilling their plans for their new possession.

Their aim was not really to establish an Arab domain, but to build an Italian society, a 'fourth shore' for Italy.[8] As far as they knew, Libya's only exploitable resource was agriculture, and the fascist government aimed to fill the country with small farmers imported from the mainland. Libya did indeed go through a rapid process of modernization, in both urban development and communications. More than 30,000 enthusiastic settlers moved there in the course of the 1930s. By the end of the decade, the total Italian population exceeded 100,000. Libya was to be a fully integrated part of Italy, similar to Algeria's integration into France, and was not to be ruled as a colony.

This Italian dream was not to have a long life. When Italy joined World War II in 1940, the Libyan–Egyptian border formed a frontline. Graziani attacked British-controlled Egypt, but was beaten back by British forces which occupied Cyrenaica twice in the first two years of the war. They won a decisive victory against the Axis forces at Tobruk in 1942, and moved westwards towards Tripoli. Free French forces moved at the same time into the Fezzan from French West Africa, which had remained loyal to de Gaulle, and the Allies jointly put an end to Italian rule in Libya, which had thus lasted less than twelve years.

But what were the victors then to do with Libya? For the remainder of the war, the British and the French each ruled over the part of the country that they had occupied.[9] At the end of the war in 1945, they handed the issue over to the new United Nations organization. The victorious powers had divergent interests in this issue. Their first inclination was to divide Libya into its constituent parts; after all, it had only been united into one 'country' by Graziani's victory over the Sanūsīs in 1931. The British could have Cyrenaica and the French wanted the Fezzan which bordered on their West African colony; Tripolitania could be handed back to a new and democratic Italian republic, all three being 'mandated' to lead each region to an ulterior self-rule. This plan was defeated by only a small margin in the UN General Assembly in 1949. However, the mood turned quickly in the direction of 'the nations' rights to independence'. Britain came to support independence, and allowed their ally Muḥammad Idrīs al-Sanūsī, who had throughout been the recognized head of the anti-Italian resistance, to establish an 'emirate' in Cyrenaica. The French did not favour this idea, due to their strategic West African interests. However, the USA supported independence, and the UN gave their representative Adrian Pelt the job of constructing Libya's future structure of government.

Shaykh, now *amīr*, Idrīs was in fact the only leader of any national stature in Libya, and thus the clear candidate for a Libyan monarchy. He was certainly a man of Cyrenaica, the less populated eastern region, and the Sanūsī brotherhood also had extensive support in Fezzan in the south, which was also fairly thinly populated. Opinions were rather more mixed in Tripolitania, where many favoured a republic and others felt little attachment to the distant eastern regions. In spite of these strong reservations, the result was that Libya was established as a constitutional and federal kingdom, in which the three provinces should have fairly vague powers. Idrīs was, on 24 December, 1951 declared King of Libya, and it thus became the first of the four Maghreb countries to achieve independence.

The Algerian war of liberation

Libya was thus handed its independence on a silver platter from the UN, primarily because the big powers did not see any interest in the country beyond the geo-strategic, which a friendly king could easily satisfy. The situation was completely different in neighbouring Algeria, which was the last of the four to gain independence.

The French were in full control of Algeria at the turn of the century, and the Arabs had been pushed to the margins of society.[10] Many of the peasants who had lost their land moved to the towns and entered a working class that grew to perhaps half a million people. There was not enough work for all who came, so many remained unemployed and marginalized. Many, perhaps 300,000, left to find work in France, particularly after 1910. The remittances from the expatriates became an important source of income for the non-European society in Algeria.

There was little political activity among Arabs or Berbers in the first decades after the 1871 Mukranī rebellion. The former tribal leaders and notables had died, been neutralized or were torn away from the social context that gave them influence. The French central government in Paris saw the need to build a new, modernized leadership for the '*indigènes*' by giving them education, but attempts in that direction were efficiently sabotaged by the settlers, whose view was that 'if education was to become widespread, then the natives would shout in unison, "Algeria to the Arabs!"'

However, the nationalities law of 1889 had given some '*assimilés*' the opportunity to apply for French citizenship if they cut all ties to Arabic or Muslim culture. A few hundred took this opportunity. The authorities also established some local administration councils where the Muslims were allowed to elect some members from their ranks. This was a tiny sliver of influence, but it gave rise to some early requests for reform. Their main demand was to have the draconian *indigénat* law abolished (this only happened in 1946). Following the earlier Ottoman and Tunisian reformists, they called themselves the Young Algerians, but they differed from them in that the Algerians were not rooted in the traditional upper class. They were also strong adherents of assimilation into French society and rejected any idea of Algerian separatism. The main spokesman, Farḥāt ʿAbbās, wrote that 'there is no Algerian nation'. Instead, they aimed at abolishing all discrimination, so that Arabs and Berbers could become just as French as the other inhabitants in the society.

This was, however, completely out of the question for the settlers, and they were able to block any attempt from Paris to consider the requests for greater integration. So, as they met complete rejection from the French side, the assimilationist tendency remained weak.

The starting point for Algerian nationalism can be put at the 1930 centennial celebrations of the French invasion. The trend grew from two different directions.[11] One was a religious movement that was at first strictly apolitical. Muḥammad ʿAbduh's ideas about Islamic reform (*salafīya*) had struck a chord with many religious leaders in Algeria. The most prominent among the reformers was ʿAbd al-Ḥamīd Ben Bādīs, who had been educated at the Zaytūna in Tunisia. He criticized the traditional religious leadership that did not want to engage with society, and established an 'Association of ʿ*ulamāʾ* [religious scholars]' with the aim of promoting Muslim education. They built a series of schools based on modern reformed Islamic theology, which would also teach modern subjects.

Ben Bādīs also attacked 'false superstitions' among the Muslims, aiming mainly at the Sufi brotherhoods that still dominated popular Islam in the region. As we have seen, Sufi brotherhoods had on crucial occasions been politically active, such as in the anti-colonial resistance from the time of ʿAbd al-Qādir forwards: But these were exceptions: most brotherhoods stayed away from politics, and the Salafi reformist view of ʿAbduh, as well as Ben Bādīs and others, saw these popular movements as tainted with non-Islamic and outdated beliefs in the supernatural powers of holy men. Instead of worshipping saints and praying at their graves for miracles, Muslims should seek a rational and progressive understanding of Islam that emphasized how all men were equal before God and gained His favour through their own acts. In this way, Ben Bādīs's reformists were at odds with the traditional ʿ*ulamāʾ*, who were heavily imbued with popular Sufism. But because of the weakening of traditional Muslim society, there were not many such traditional ʿ*ulamāʾ* of note in Algeria, and they played no significant political role. Thus, Ben Bādīs and his reformists came to represent the religious element in Algeria.

His movement was not to have any political agenda, and Ben Bādīs at first appeared to favour the French 'protection' of Algeria. But the absence of reforms made him turn more and more towards political activism in the course of the 1930s. Thus, he wrote an influential answer to Farḥāt ʿAbbās's article on 'no Algerian nation'. He stated that 'the Muslim population is not part of France, cannot be part of France and does not wish to be part of France'. In 1938, the settlers were able to force Ben Bādīs's schools to close, and from that moment he became fully committed to political activism. His ʿ*ulamāʾ* association became an important strand of Algerian nationalism, in contrast to ʿAbbās's more moderate current.

The third current of Algerian Arab politics was anything but moderate, and was formed not in Algeria, but among the Algerian immigrant workers in France. The pro-communist trade union for North Africans, *Étoile Nord-Africaine*, had been established by the Algerian Messali Hadj (Maṣṣālī al-Ḥājj) in 1926. Ten years later, it established a section in Algeria, and in the following year this union became the Algerian People's Party (PPA). These 'Messalists' argued openly for independence, and although the PPA distanced itself from the communists, it was the strongest advocate for radical politics both in nationalist and in social issues. In the course of the 1930s, the Messalists drew increasing support and became a dominant voice among the growing numbers of politically active Algerians.

In 1936, Léon Blum's United Front government tried in Algeria, as in the other Maghreb countries, to reform French policies.[12] Its most important efforts here were to expand the number of Muslims with the right to vote, and to extend the influence of their elected representatives. There were still separate elections for French citizens and *indigènes*, but the latter were now to get equal say with the settlers in the election of town mayors. But, again, the settlers were able to kill the suggestion of reform. Blum could not ignore this important group of voters and withdrew his proposal, to the great disappointment of ʿAbbās and his assimilationists. This was perhaps the last realistic opportunity the French had to make the two groups of Algerians, French and Muslim, join into a united Algeria under French rule. After this defeat, even ʿAbbās began to move away from the idea of 'becoming French' and closer to ideas of Arab self-rule.

Self-rule could mean either complete independence and separation or an internal autonomy in alliance with France. The Messalists were definite adherents of the first option, while both Ben Bādīs and later ʿAbbās, for a long time, favoured the second. World War II, when it came four years later, had much the same effect in Algeria as in its two neighbouring countries: a certain amount of satisfaction in the defeat of the colonial power, but none of the nationalist leaders came to support Vichy or the Axis powers. The invasion of the outspokenly anti-colonialist Americans in 1942 gave rise to widespread hopes here, as among the neighbours, but de Gaulle was not forthcoming except for some promises of reform. He did finally abolish the discriminatory *indigénat* laws and gave the Muslim local representatives some extended influence, but this was far from satisfying the Muslim opinion, while it led to unrest among the settlers.

The situation grew more tense, and large demonstrations broke out when Messali Hadj was deported in May 1945. On 8 May, V-Day in Europe, protesters attacked the European quarters in Sétif and some neighbouring towns and killed over 100 French civilians. This led to a violent response: a rapidly assembled militia of *colons* supported by the air force massacred more than 6–8,000 Algerians in the days that followed.

Paris sought to ease the tension with new reform proposals, but these went too far for the settlers and were inadequate for the nationalists. There was no longer any question of assimilation; the discussion among the nationalists now turned around what Algeria's future status should be. Farḥāt ʿAbbās still favoured a more moderate approach and suggested an independent Algeria as part of a 'commonwealth' with France, while the Messalists wanted a clean and total break. In 1947, Paris suggested an 'equal participation' between Muslims and settlers in the government of Algeria, but the time for such proposals had passed long ago on the nationalist side, while the settlers called it 'dishonourable'; it was rejected by all.

The most radical nationalists instead began to plan for direct action, inspired by developments in other French colonies. A group of activists from the Messalist party, among them Aḥmed Ben Bella, Hocine Ait Aḥmad and Muḥammad Boudiaf, began to prepare a secret force for the liberation of Algeria, supported in particular by Nasser in Egypt.

By 1954, the weakness of the French colonial empire became evident with the defeat at Dien Bien Phu in May. The new Algerian movement struck six months later. On 1 November 1954, it carried out a series of terrorist attacks in various parts of Algeria under the name of the *Front de Libération Nationale*, FLN.[13]

The Front was at this point fairly small, but it caught the French unawares, and the army was not able to put an end to its attacks. Instead, the authorities responded with harsh measures that hurt wide sections of the Muslim population. This, aided by deliberate provocations from the FLN, led to increased polarization of Algerian society. The FLN came more and more to be seen as heroes for liberation, while the resentment against the ever more brutal French soldiers turned to hatred. This was to give the FLN a solid political base, even though it was always militarily inferior to the forces the French were able to put into the field.

The increased polarization of society made most nationalist groups join the FLN front, and in 1956 they established a transitional government, GPRA, in exile in Cairo. The old assimilationist Farḥāt ʿAbbās was given the position of honour as President, and the ʿ*ulamāʾ* (whose historical leader Ben Bādīs had died in 1940) were given significant positions. Only Messali Hadj himself and his closest followers stayed away and formed a competing guerrilla group, mostly because of personal conflicts.

Paris used all means at its disposal to defeat the rebellion, including a number of oppressive measures against the civilian population. But they also tried to find a negotiated solution. However, these efforts failed when an aeroplane with most of the FLN leadership, including Ben Bella, Ait Aḥmad and Boudiaf, was caught by the French air force and the three were put in prison.

Instead, the FLN extended its war using both regular rural guerrillas and urban warfare with terror bombings, of which the 'Battle of Algiers' was particularly important and lasted for several months in 1957. The oppressive French policies met with little support internationally, against a growing anti-colonialist world opinion, US scepticism and a growing number of reports of French torture and counter-terrorism. In France, opposing the war in Algeria became important for the political left and centre, while the right remained sympathetic to the settlers who fought for 'the glory of France'.

The war remained at the centre stage of French politics, and eventually caused the fall of the fourth French republic. The Algerian settlers and their supporters in France felt that the parliamentary system could only lead to weak and changing governments that did not have the solidity to defeat the rebellion. A strong man must take over. The President finally gave in to their pressure and called on the hero of the French liberation in the world war, General de Gaulle, to take his position. He accepted, but only if he was given the opportunity to create a more presidential system with a shift of executive powers from the Parliament to the President. This was accepted, and de Gaulle thus initiated what is today called the fifth French republic.

However, he did not fulfil the settlers' hopes. From his military background, he saw that the war against the guerrillas could not be won by arms and that a political solution must be found. He thus approached the FLN with an offer of autonomy. This was insufficient for the FLN and they rejected both this offer and several others that de Gaulle made in the course of the following years. On the opposite side, these talks with the rebels fuelled discontent among the settlers. One of their leaders, General Salan, attempted a *coup d'état* in 1960, but was quickly defeated. Instead, the extremist settlers established a secret army, the OAS, which was to combat both the FLN and the French 'defeatists'. They made several attempts on the life of the 'traitor' de Gaulle, but without success.

FLN stuck to their demands, but were unable to create any military breakthrough, and the population began to grow weary of the war that seemed to be going nowhere. In 1961, de Gaulle called for a referendum on a proposal for independence. The FLN called for a boycott, but the voters ignored this and came out in great numbers to accept the proposal. At this point, the FLN withdrew its opposition to formal negotiations, and the GPRA and France met in Évian in Switzerland. In 1962, they reached an agreement that Algeria should get full independence if the people supported it in a vote. A referendum was held later in the year, with more than 90 per cent in favour of independence.

In return, the French population should, according to the Évian agreement, have certain guarantees. They should be allowed to choose between French and Algerian citizenship, and their French language and culture should be protected. But these sections became dead letters, as the vast majority of the French population, then about one million strong, fled in a great rush to France in the following months. Many had lived in Algeria for generations and had little connection to the mainland. They became known as *pieds-noirs* ('black-feet') and came to a country that had little awareness of and little sympathy for their situation, not least because the OAS had also carried out terrorist attacks in France.

The situation was far worse for the more than 200,000 Algerians who had chosen to side with France and fought on their side, the *ḥarkī*s. They were not allowed to enter France, and those who were smuggled into the country were placed in camps for many years. Those left behind in Algeria bore the brunt of a bloody revenge: perhaps as many as 100,000 *ḥarkīs* were massacred in the months following independence. The bitterness of this reckoning may also have influenced the ferocity of combat in many areas thirty years later, when Algeria was again in the grip of civil war. The war of liberation was in general a very bloody affair, with great brutality on all sides. The French lost thousands of civilians, while somewhere between half a million and a million Algerians lost their lives, and large parts of the country were laid waste.

6

INDEPENDENCE

AUTHORITY AND MODERNITY

Tunisia: a monarchic republic

It was Bourguiba's combination of pragmatism and the ability to mobilize opinion that made the transition to independence so peaceful in Tunisia. He was rewarded with deep gratitude by the people and was seen as the 'father of the nation', a sentiment that lasted the rest of his life. Tunisians flocked around the *mujāhid al-akbar*, the 'greatest liberation fighter', as he was called, and by and large accepted that he came to see himself as the only person capable of running the country.[1]

However, the unanimity was not total. There was opposition to his personalized rule and to his political project. It was most pronounced at the beginning of his reign, and came from within his own party. During Bourguiba's years of exile in Egypt, the party had been run by the general secretary Ṣālaḥ ben Yūsuf, who had expanded the party's base and also formed a political following of his own, in particular in his native Jerba and surrounding districts in the south of the country. Thus, he had become a potential rival for Bourguiba when the latter returned to Tunisia in 1949, and Ben Yūsuf was pushed aside. He consequently began to criticize Bourguiba, at first from the left, saying that the party had given the French too much in the negotiations; later, he changed his tack and attacked Bourguiba from the right.

The conflict between the two was personal, but they also had different political worldviews. They came from different backgrounds and had dissimilar plans for Tunisia. Bourguiba was an unbridled modernist; he had benefited from a French education and aimed to bring Tunisia into the world he knew from his time in Europe. He recognized that Tunisia had an Islamic past and a Muslim character, but was uninterested in religion and 'old-fashioned' culture. The retrograde social structures of Tunisia were holding it back and had to be broken as quickly as possible.

Ben Yūsuf was much more open to the religious factor, and wanted to combine modernization with a defence of Tunisia's Arab character. He was thus close to the traditional religious elite, and his supporters, the 'Yusufists', primarily became proponents for an Islamic opposition to the Europeanization they felt Bourguiba was favouring. These ideas had appeal among more conservative circles in the countryside and in the south, and there developed serious clashes between the Yusufists and the police just before independence was declared in 1956. The country was for a moment on the brink of civil war, and parts of the earlier *fallāgha* guerrilla movement were ready to join Ben Yūsuf in a challenge to Bourguiba's power.

However, the large majority of the population rejected this attack on the hero of the liberation, and Ben Yūsuf had to give up his attempt. He left Tunisia for Egypt in January 1957, and was murdered there four years later. His rebellion died with him, and Bourguiba and the Neo-Destour won the 1959 elections unopposed. Nevertheless, the danger of a Yūsufist rising remained into the 1960s.

The conservative Yūsufists were not the only section of the Neo-Destour that had a political agenda independent of the leader. A second challenge, from the left this time, also had roots in the dark years in the late 1940s when the party had been under such pressure. Then, the trade union UGTT had carried the nationalist torch, and they felt after independence that this gave them the right to an autonomous voice in the political debate. Their purpose was to protect the rights of their members and of the working classes in general. Thus, the UGTT and their leader, Aḥmad ben Ṣālaḥ, demanded economic reforms that could turn the country in a more socialist direction. But in Bourguiba's political system there could not be more than one power centre. He therefore intervened in the UGTT and, using his tremendous personal popularity and authority, made the congress depose ben Ṣālaḥ and turned the trade union into a powerless organ for Neo-Destour policies.

Neo-Destour now meant Bourguiba. He was the head of the state, the party and the government.[2] There was no opposition in Parliament, and all major decisions were made by the party and its leadership. Party and state merged to such an extent that Bourguiba never bothered to establish municipal councils after the French-led administration had left. Instead, the local branches of the Neo-Destour party took over the municipal administration, and of course these local branches only implemented the decisions made by the party leadership.

Bourguiba initiated far-reaching processes of modernization in the country. He developed a school system where French and Arabic were used as languages of instruction, and particularly French in higher education. He modernized agriculture and other sectors of the economy. About half of the European settlers left Tunisia in the course of the first three years of independence, and their properties were taken over by the state. Their land was turned into commercial farms, and this was expanded when the state also took control of the land holdings of the *waqf* religious foundations (in the Maghreb known as *ḥabūs*). The *waqfs* were economically important in themselves, but it was even more important that they formed the primary economic basis for the *ʿulamāʾ*, who had opposed Bourguiba's programme and in part supported the Yūsufists. The loss of the *ḥabūs* land weakened this religious class even further, and they were virtually without any influence from the 1960s onwards.

Bourguiba also addressed the role of religion directly. He never went as far as Turkey's Atatürk in attacking Islam head-on. Instead, he always insisted that his reforms of religion were within the confines of accepted theology through the process of interpretation, *ijtihād*, and thus were properly Islamic. He was also able to get loyal religious scholars to support his changes. Thus, he abolished the remaining Muslim courts and introduced a new family law which banned polygamy and gave husband and wife equal access to divorce, but also put the burden of supporting the family equally on man and wife.[3] However, his attempts in 1960 to abolish the Muslim Ramaḍān fast failed. He argued that the fasting, which every year made the economy slow down for a month, hampered the development of the country. This was a peaceful *jihād* of recovery, he said, and in Islamic theology fasting can be suspended for those who fight in a *jihād*. But this line of argument was not accepted by the scholars nor understood by the people, and the Ramaḍān fast took place as usual, both that year and thereafter.

Bourguiba was hardly a great pan-Arabist, but he did support the FLN in their war in Algeria.[4] This caused increased tension with France, which still had some military bases in Tunisia. In 1961, Bourguiba organized a march on the French naval base at Bizerte. The ensuing fighting resulted in a few dead on the French side and many more among the Tunisians. At this time, France's international standing in North Africa was so low that de Gaulle found it politic to pull the last French forces out of Tunisia two years later.

While Bourguiba thus stood up to France, he provoked his Arab neighbours by taking a fairly passive attitude on the Palestinian issue. He was an early proponent of talks with Israel, and few in the fairly large community of Tunisian Jews found reason to leave the country in the first years after independence. However, the 1967 Arab–Israeli war sparked widespread anti-Israeli demonstrations in Tunisia, and at this point many Jews left Tunisia for Israel, as did many Jews from Morocco. But a substantial number remained in both countries, and their presence may have been a reason why the two countries have always been among the Arab states with the most relaxed attitude towards Israel.

Tunisia's political system has shown an unbroken continuity from independence in 1956 through the half-century that followed until 2011, with only two presidents. But the country still passed through several politically distinct periods. The one that stands out the most is the 'socialist' period of the 1960s.

It was primarily socialist in the sense of promoting state-sponsored capitalism, whereas private property itself was never put in question. Bourguiba's main aim was to modernize the economy as quickly as possible and, like many rulers in the region in the 1950s, he believed that the state must be the engine to further economic growth. Thus, he brought the left-wing former trade unionist leader Aḥmad ben Ṣālaḥ into his government. ben Ṣālaḥ became a 'super-minister' charged with constructing a planned economy where state interventions should lead to rapid industrialization and a modernization of agriculture. He began an ambitious programme with large investments. 'Socialism' became the party's new slogan, and it changed its name from 'Neo-Destour' to the 'Socialist Destour Party', PSD.

However, although there was considerable growth in the economy, ben Ṣālaḥ was not able to satisfy the expectations for a rapid transformation. More and more sectors began to fall behind plan in the course of the 1960s. Many in the party also disliked the new socialist rhetoric. What finally caused the fall of socialism was a plan to create large state-owned collective farms. The big landowners protested vehemently. Bourguiba had never been ideologically committed to any particular system, and pragmatically saw that the socialist way had reached a dead end. Thus, he fired ben Ṣālaḥ in 1970 and charged him with treason (for not having followed the President's wishes). ben Ṣālaḥ fled the country and, even though he remained a voice of leftist opposition from his exile, his following had thus lost its influence in Tunisian politics. The only way to be heard in Tunisia was through Bourguiba. He alone made the decisions.

So, the political current switched over to the liberalist side from the 1970s. The state-owned sector remained very large, but the new government opened up the economy to foreign investors as well as domestic. This had a positive effect, and economic growth took off in the 1970s.[5]

All sections of society gained from the economic developments, but some gained more than others. Economic liberalization led, here as elsewhere, to greater social inequality, and as the divisions grew deeper, murmurs spread among the workers. The trade union movement, UGTT, so far a loyal instrument to the party, now tried to loosen the ties by harnessing this discontent and calling for a general strike in 1978. The strike was brutally suppressed by the police in what became known as 'Black Thursday'. The UGTT was crushed as a political force.

Still, these events caused some political developments. The governing party, PSD, had never been seriously challenged, and had in fact been the only legal party since 1963. Now some independent groups were allowed to organize, although none of them gained much influence and the PSD in effect remained the single governing party.

On the left, Aḥmad Mestīrī, a former prime minister under the PSD, sought to organize a social democratic alternative. A few centrist or liberal groups also tried to establish themselves. But all these new leaders had a background in the PSD, and could not credibly present themselves as a distinct alternative. Only Mestīrī's group were able to win more than 1 or 2 per cent of the vote.

More significant was the rise of political Islam. This was not a continuation of the old Yusufist trend, which had been dead for almost two decades; and the new groups were not based on the traditionalist religious circles. Instead, the new 'Islamic Tendency' (MTI) was led by a young and well-educated generation with Rashīd Ghannūshī as their foremost thinker.[6] He was inspired by the Muslim Brotherhood in Egypt, and favoured internal reform of Islam and a greater role for a modernized religion in politics and society. They thus rejected Bourguiba's secular state and sought to promote a new morality based on the faith. But although they were clearly part of the new Islamist trend that appeared in many Arab countries, Ghannūshī and the MTI are still normally seen as perhaps the most moderate voice in modern Islamism.

Still, their programme was unacceptable in Tunisia's political system, and positions hardened both on the government's side and among the Islamists. Ghannūshī's rhetoric took a sharper tone and the party was in 1987 accused of planning a *coup d'état.* Ghannūshī and several other leaders were condemned to death in a lower court. This caused widespread unrest, and in the following year led to bomb attacks in Sousse and in Monastir, Bourguiba's home town. Things were sliding out of control.

These events took place in a period of increasing chaos in the political system. Bourguiba's health had been declining during the course of the 1970s, and in particular into the 1980s. His illnesses forced him to stay abroad frequently and for long periods. But he insisted on taking every important decision himself, which caused increasing problems during his many absences. His mental health also worsened, and he could waver from one view to the next, fire one minister and then another, often without apparent reason. His increasing unpredictability brought politics to a standstill, waiting for him to make up his mind. Clearly, the situation was becoming untenable.

In one of his sudden about-turns, Bourguiba in 1987 promoted the head of the security police, Zayn al-ʿĀbidīn Ben ʿAlī, to Prime Minister. The unrest of the Ghannūshī crisis gave the latter the opportunity to seize the initiative, when Bourguiba started insisting that Ghannūshī should die, an action that might have ripped the country apart. Ben ʿAlī had the President declared medically incapable of carrying out his job and took over his position. Bourguiba was, under protest, confined to one of his palaces, and was kept there until he died all of 13 years later in 2000, at the age of 97.[7]

Although he took power in what amounted to a coup, Ben ʿAlī continued the political line set out by Bourguiba and must largely be seen as continuing Bourguiba's regime. His removal of the sick President was generally accepted as a necessity, and he took over all Bourguiba's authority as supreme leader of the country at the head of his party. However, he changed its name, removing the now outdated 'socialist' label: it became the 'Democratic Destour Assembly', RCD.

Ben ʿAlī set aside Ghannūshī's death penalty and gave the opposition parties, including the Islamists, a bit more space in which to operate. Ghannūshī converted the MTI to a party called *al-Nahḍa*, the Awakening, to circumvent a ban on parties based on religion. That was not sufficient to have it recognized as a formal party, but its candidates were allowed to stand as independents in the parliamentary elections of 1989. They turned out to be the only opposition force able win a noticeable number of votes, gaining 15 per cent. Ben ʿAlī's RCD took most of the rest, and with 80 per cent got all the seats in parliament. Ben ʿAlī was confirmed as President in an unopposed election shortly after.

This demonstrated that there was no more room for a real opposition force under Ben ʿAlī than there had been under Bourguiba, and Ghannūshī chose to leave the country and settle in exile in London. The events in Algeria soon allowed Ben ʿAlī to start a campaign against Nahḍa and the Islamists. Their party was suppressed; the leaders who had not left the country were arrested; and the party never again had the chance to organize during his presidency. Fear of an Algerian-style confrontation made many Tunisians support this restrictive policy. From exile, Ghannūshī continued developing his ideas of a modernized and reformist type of Islamism and, in spite of the repression, his voice of opposition probably remained the one with the greatest resonance in the country towards the end of the century.

One factor that hampered the development of Islamism, and certainly of a more radical Islamism as seen in other Middle Eastern countries, was the economic growth that benefited most

Tunisians. Ben ʿAlī allowed for more economic liberalization, and many state-owned enterprises were privatized. Tunisia signed a trade agreement with the EU. This forced them to implement a series of severe austerity measures, but the economy still enjoyed healthy growth in this period. This gave Tunisians the highest standard of living in the Maghreb, and has, after half a century of social modernization, made them probably feel closer to Europe than many of their neighbours. However, the political situation was still marked by draconian authoritarianism. Using the danger of Islamism as an excuse, Ben ʿAlī suppressed any voice of dissent, not just Islamic but also secular leftists or liberals of any kind, and the regime became more and more isolated from large sections of society.

Independent Morocco and royal power

Tunisia under Bourguiba may be called a 'monarchic republic', since the President ruled as an autocrat. The new Morocco that emerged from the French protectorate was a real monarchy, a royal power where the King personally made all decisions himself and personified political rule in the same way as Bourguiba did in his republic.[8] But there were clear differences between these two autocracies, and it may be said that Muḥammad V had to work harder to establish a personal rule for himself than did Bourguiba to establish his monopoly of power.

An important difference was that Bourguiba could build his system around a mass party, the Neo-Destour. The Moroccan King had no similar political instrument. The largest nationalist party, Istiqlāl, had objectives of their own, and their leader ʿAllāl al-Fāsī had a personal popularity and legitimacy on a par with the King from his role in the independence struggle. Istiqlāl was a heterogeneous party, where a strong left wing under Mehdī Ben Barka worked with expanding labour unions to promote a left-leaning policy.

However, the first problem that the new kingdom faced was the 'liberation army', the self-styled body of guerrillas that remained active, particularly in Berber areas in northern Morocco. They rejected the authority of the Istiqlāl government and were loyal only to the King in person. The group had a radical nationalist agenda, but its support was strong in traditional rural areas that distrusted the urban middle-class party, Istiqlāl. They also disliked what they considered to be an 'Arabist' policy that did not take the Berber population properly into account.

In order to channel the energy of this 'liberation army', which strictly speaking had not done much actual liberating, in a less divisive direction, the King requested that it should take part in the liberation of the south still under Spanish control. Morocco's pre-colonial borders towards the south and south-east had always been vague, and the kingdom now claimed much of the desert regions all the way down to the Senegal river. This included not just the regions under Spanish control, but also south-western Algeria and large chunks of French West Africa, present-day Mauritania and parts of Mali. The new 'liberation army for Sahara' was able to make Spain give up a minor Spanish-controlled area called Tarfaya in southern Morocco, but was otherwise unsuccessful in pressing Moroccan claims. However, Morocco maintained its formal claims to these territories, ensuring that its relations with its neighbours remained distant for several decades.

Following this campaign, the King asked the liberation army to depose its arms; and most of them complied, many entering the new national army. Here they joined officers and soldiers who had fought for the French in the protectorate army. The armed forces were to a large degree recruited from traditional social groups and were always distant to the Istiqlāl and the other new parties from the same urban middle class. Instead, the military became the most important basis for the King's power. The crown Prince, Ḥasan, was made Commander-in-Chief of the army, strengthening his identification with it. The King's closest ally in the armed forces was General Muḥammad Oufkir, a conservative with a Berber background who had supported the King since the 1940s.

The Istiqlāl dominated the government in the first period after independence, and Ben Barka was able to nationalize many resources taken from the old *qāʾid* families that had sided with France. Both the Glāwīs and the Kattānīs lost much of their land. However, as their common goal of independence had been achieved, the various currents within the nationalist party began to go their separate ways. Tensions arose between the supporters of the two dominant personalities, the leftist Ben Barka and the more conservative al-Fāsī. The King played into this game by giving his support to Ben Barka. Thus, when Ben Barka broke away from Istiqlāl in 1959 to form his own nationalist party, UNFP, the King made him Prime Minister, as it was the King's prerogative to appoint the government.

This became typical of the palace way of playing politics. By alternately supporting left-wing and right-wing parties without any apparent regard for their ideologies, the King was able to balance the political forces against each other and make them all dependent on his support, ensuring their basic loyalty to his personal monarchic power. The alternation of power also tended to favour moderation on all sides; when the UNFP came into government, they jettisoned the more radical elements and moved towards the centre.

King Muḥammad V, the symbol of the liberation struggle, died in 1961. His son, Ḥasan II, had by then been actively involved in governing the country for many years, and the transition was smooth. He had, like his father, legitimacy from the palace's role in the fight for independence, and from his partially religious role as 'commander of the faithful', *amīr al-muʾminīn*, which the ʿAlawī sultans and kings had claimed since the seventeenth century and which many religious Moroccans took very seriously.

However, Morocco's economy still had problems, and social unrest grew in the course of the 1960s.[9] There were large student demonstrations in 1965. The King, who at this moment worked with an Istiqlāl government, changed tack again and asked Ben Barka to return from France, where he had been in exile for a time. He hoped that placing the left in government would stave off unrest in the trade unions. This strategy did not find favour among the King's traditional supporters. His 'right-hand man', General Oufkir, feared that a left-wing government would damage the interests of the more prosperous classes, and arranged that Ben Barka was murdered in Paris before he could return. Thus, the King's turn to the left was aborted, as the UNFP accused the King (and de Gaulle) of the murder, and refused to cooperate.

The army had thus started to see itself as an independent political actor, and the tension between it and the palace became even more dramatic a few years later. In 1971, a group of young officers attempted a *coup d'état* and took the King prisoner in his Skhirat palace. But they were unwilling to murder him, and the King was able to escape and defeat the rebellion. Oufkir sided with the King, and remained in his post. But there was no doubt that he was behind a second coup attempt that took place the following year. Air force fighters attacked the King's private aircraft and nearly made it crash. However, for the second time the King 'miraculously' survived and this coup failed as well. Oufkir committed suicide, while the King's authority was bolstered through the manner in which he had come through these coup attempts.

But it was clear that the weakening of support for the King in his own military power base was a warning of more serious problems in society. No one dared to attack or criticize the King directly, and those who did were quickly shipped off to prison or a lunatic asylum. But the increasing unrest caused by the economic problems could still over time put the King's power in jeopardy.

So the King, like his father, sought to defuse a difficult situation by turning public attention southwards. Spain had, after the fall of the Franco regime in 1974, begun to pull out of its last colonial territories, among them 'Spanish Sahara', Ṣaqīyat al-Ḥamrāʾ and Rio del Oro.[10] Both Morocco in the north and Mauritania in the south immediately claimed this territory, while an independence movement, Polisario, declared a separate

Saharan Republic. The King made this into an issue of patriotism and national honour and organized a 'green march' in which thousands of civilian and unarmed Moroccans marched across the border and 'liberated' this southern section of 'historical Morocco'. This was a tremendous political success: patriotic fervour was strong, and the King used the Sahara issue to reinforce national unity around his own person. As the conflict turned into open war with Polisario, it got to be more and more difficult to raise opposition against the King, even on domestic issues or questions of his autocratic rule, and the King thus reaffirmed his power.

This did not solve the economic problems, however, and there was serious unrest in Casablanca in 1981. But the situation improved in some economic sectors in the course of the 1980s, and the middle class in particular saw a marked rise in their living standards. Many Morocccans also left to look for work in Europe, particularly in France and Spain. Foreign investments in Morocco increased, particularly after the government implemented more liberalist economic policies in the late 1990s.

There was little opposition to the King's power after the Sahara crisis. The generation of politicians who had an independent legitimacy from the liberation struggle, such as al-Fāsī and Ben Barka, had passed away. Politicians and parties vied for the changeable favour of the King in the hope of a place in government, whatever their politics. When the socialist front of USFP, a left-wing split from the UNFP, increased their support in the 1998 parliamentary elections, they were asked to form the government. But little changed in the actual policies carried out, as these were in any case decided by the King.

As in the rest of the Middle East, it was the Islamist currents that presented the clearest political alternative. But they did not constitute any substantial challenge to the regime in Morocco. Several minor Islamic groups accepted the basis for political participation, which was to avoid any challenge to the King and his power, and they posed less of a radical alternative to the existing parties. The only group of significance that broke with this basis was *al-ʿAdl wa'l-iḥsān* (Justice and Piety), founded by ʿAbd al-Salām Yāsīn.[11] He published in 1974 an 'open letter' where he strongly attacked the King for letting Morocco become a country of infidelity (*jāhilīya*). He was therefore interned in an insane asylum for some years. After his release, his movement was largely tolerated on condition that it refrained from extremist activism. Yāsīn thus became the 'Islamist voice' in Morocco, but without the structured organization typical of other Islamist movements.

He was also different from most Islamists in coming from a Sufi background,[12] while most Islamist currents reject Sufism as superstition. The major issue for Moroccan Islamists was the King's role as *amīr al-muʾminīn*, commander of the faithful, a religious as well as a political title. Islamist movements often consider this an ideal model for Muslim rule and one of the elements that makes a country an 'Islamic state'. If one accepts that the Moroccan king is such a commander, and most Moroccan Muslims did so, then it becomes a religious duty to follow his commands. This made it difficult to gain support for a radical Islamist challenge to the monarchy. Yāsīn rejected the King's right to this title, and the movement has proposed a republican government instead.

In the late 1990s, greater political liberalization allowed Islamist forces to stand in elections, and a new and more moderate Islamist party, 'Justice and Development', PDJ, made striking gains. It accepts the King's role and can thus participate fully in political life. It has become the dominant opposition force in parliament, while Yāsīn's movement, now with his daughter Nādiya as an important spokesperson, remains a significant force outside established politics.

The most heated topic of conflict between Islamists, traditionalists and modernists, has—here as elsewhere in the Muslim world—been family law. Morocco had in 1958 introduced a new family law that reformed some elements of marriage and divorce, but was still predominantly within the traditional Sharīʿa framework, allowing polygamy, the husband's paramount right to divorce, and so on. In 1992, the King raised the question of revising this law with the aim of giving women more rights. The proposal eventually put forward by the law commission went far in removing the Sharīʿa influence in these fields, which led to heated debates and mobilization both for and against.[13] It gained vociferous support both from women's groups and from modernist and liberal currents generally, while the religious and traditional sectors rejected it. Both sides organized mass demonstrations in major cities, the opponents perhaps having the edge in numbers. Thus, it fell to the King to decide whether he should accept or reject the new law.

However, King Ḥasan did not get to make this choice. He died in 1999, and his son Muḥammad VI inherited the throne. The new King kept a more withdrawn profile than his father, but eventually sided with the liberals on the family law issue, and the new law that was passed in 2004 went almost as far as the Tunisian one in improving the position of women in legal matters. However, it fell short of full gender equality, and it was marked by redefining the meaning of traditional Sharīʿa concepts to allow women's participation, rather than to replace them completely with secular terms. But the liberals viewed it as a victory, and the traditionalists as a defeat.

The King was, on the whole, perceived as a more modern monarch and made some reforms.[14] He removed the perennial minister of the interior, Driss Baṣrī, who had served in all governments, irrespective of party colour, since Oufkir's time and was seen as the real power in the country and the old King's instrument. However, hopes for more drastic changes were dashed. The King made small steps towards reform, but by and large maintained the political system inherited from his father.

Morocco had always been a pro-Western country in international politics, and was particularly close to the United States. Relations with France also improved after the end of the Algerian war. Morocco had more problems with its neighbours than with the world powers. Algeria had always been a rival, in spite of Morocco's support for the FLN during the liberation war. Morocco refused to accept the existing border between them, because they claimed that several areas in Algeria's south-west belonged historically to Morocco. The Sahara conflict also soured relations with all neighbours, even though Morocco eventually gave up its completely unrealistic claims to all of Mauritania and parts of Mali. Algeria supported Polisario, Morocco's enemy. International opinion, in particular in Africa, favoured ideas of national independence and anti-colonialism, and Polisario was able to draw on these sentiments. When the Organization of African Unity recognized Western Sahara as an independent nation, Morocco withdrew from the organization and did not return—the only African country to remain outside the new African Union.

7

STATES AND IDEOLOGIES

ALGERIA AND LIBYA

Algeria: Socialism and Islamism

The transition to independence was marked by continuity both in Morocco and in Tunisia, even though it was continuity of a traditional monarchy and upper class in Morocco and of a modernized, French-inspired middle class in Tunisia. In Algeria, however, the traditional upper class had been crushed already in the nineteenth century. There was a new middle class with nationalist spokesmen like Farḥāt ʿAbbās and Ben Bādīs, but it was small and was soon overshadowed by new social forces that were created during the liberation war itself. The transition was therefore much more of a political and social revolution than in the two other countries, and the new rulers had to construct a new society pretty much from the ground up.[1]

Algeria also teetered on the brink of civil war in the immediate aftermath of independence. There were three political 'centres' that had contributed to the liberation, and all three wanted to play a part in the new society. The historical leadership of the FLN under Ben Bella, who had been kept in a French prison since 1956, was one. The transitional government of GPRA in Cairo, which had negotiated the Évian agreement, was another. And the National Liberation Army, ALN, was a third centre. This army was divided between an 'external' leadership, which had directed the campaign from the neighbouring countries under the leadership of Houari Boumedienne, and an 'internal' front organized into various districts, often fairly independently from the national leadership.

At liberation, the GPRA moved to Algiers and became the new government. They soon came to see Boumedienne as a challenger to their authority. Ben Bella, who as head of the FLN considered himself to be the leader of the revolution, supported Boumedienne, while some parts of the 'internal' ALN supported the GPRA when it tried to remove Boumedienne from his position. Clashes broke out in the early autumn of 1962, but the GPRA did not have the political support necessary to prevail, and was dissolved. Ben Bella was thus elected the first President of Algeria in October, and the FLN became the dominant party.

The FLN saw itself in the Arab nationalist tradition of Nasser's Egypt and elsewhere. As in Egypt, Ben Bella wanted Algeria to have a single-party system under the FLN. But several of the movement's historical leaders had by now begun forming their own political currents and protested against the one-party state—among them Muḥammad Boudiaf who went into exile. The Berber communities in Kabylia were worried that the FLN would emphasize the Arab nature of Algeria over its Berber heritage, and Ait Aḥmad, another of FLN's historic leaders, broke out to form the socialist party FFS with Kabyle support. This party was banned, and he too left the country. The elderly nationalist leader Farḥāt ʿAbbās was also removed from the FLN leadership.

What remained was an alliance between Boumedienne and Ben Bella. It lasted three years. While the FLN supported Arab socialism and emphasized the economic primacy of the state, it rejected Marxism and communism. But there was a Marxist current in the movement that wanted more emphasis on combating religion and strengthening the class nature of the party. The army opposed such ideas, because they saw social stability as crucial for the development of the country. Ben Bella wavered between supporting and opposing the left, so the army deposed him in a coup in 1965 and installed Boumedienne as president. From that moment on, the army has been the determining factor in Algerian politics.

Boumedienne moved towards the political centre, but Algeria was still to have a state socialist, or rather state capitalist, economy.[2] Five-year plans were drawn up, and the state was to be the engine that drove the economy. It did have resources to put into the recovery, as the settlers had left behind considerable productive forces in their scramble to depart. These were now nationalized and turned into a significant public sector. Soon, all the property that was left behind by the French had come under state ownership. Yet, the convolutions had caused considerable problems, in particular in agriculture, and these were not completely overcome. France contributed substantial support to Algeria, but still the number of unemployed Algerians who left for France grew rapidly in the years that followed.

However, a new source of wealth appeared in the 1960s. The French had drawn the frontiers between their various colonial possessions rather haphazardly through the Sahara, so that huge empty desert tracts had been added to Algeria. Now, these regions turned out to have large oil and gas deposits. By the end of the 1960s oil and gas were Algeria's greatest export earners, and much of the income went to the state when Boumedienne nationalized the oil companies in 1971. He used the revenue to initiate an ambitious programme of industrialization with huge state-owned companies in many sectors.

The new Algeria also had to reconstruct its education system, which had been underdeveloped under French rule. The government was ideologically committed to promoting Arabic as the language of instruction and culture, but realistically had to accept that French would remain an important language in the country, and in particular in higher education. However, the ideal was to

'Arabize' the education system as quickly as possible, something that worried the Berbers, who were often competent in French and their mother tongue only, and not in literary Arabic.

Boumedienne was able to stabilize the political situation in the country, after the disruptions of the early years. The period he ruled was primarily one of economic and social reconstruction under state control. The FLN and the army, which had largely merged into one entity, were in undisputed control. By the time of Boumedienne's death in 1978 some problems in the agricultural sector had begun to cause concern, but it was his successor, Chadli Benjedid (Shādhilī ben Jadīd), who had to face the storm that was brewing.

In 1980, Berber groups began to protest against the Arabization policies and demanded cultural rights for the Berbers.[3] Later, it was the economy that caused protests. The massive state enterprises became less and less able to fulfil the expectations of increased industrial productivity, and agriculture was in no way able to keep up with the demands of a rapidly growing population. Benjedid opened the door to partial economic liberalization. This hurt the state companies, which were not prepared for competition, and caused increased unemployment. Algeria was by now completely dependent on its oil and gas exports, and the fall in the world market oil price in 1985–1986 worsened the economic crisis. Less revenue meant that the state had to reduce the subsidies on imported grain, and the price of bread rose dramatically. This hit the poorest sectors of society in particular, and widespread 'bread riots' broke out in 1988.

At the same time, the political consensus of the Boumedienne years was beginning to crack. The upper echelons of the army and industry had merged into an economic and social elite that was heavily involved in the state-run companies. Their interests were threatened by the liberalization policy, but many also defended Benjedid's reform. However, for the moment, the traditionalists dominated the leadership of the FLN. So, to broaden his political base, Benjedid abolished the one-party system and opened up political pluralism. Many of the old parties, such as

Ait Aḥmad's Berberist FFS, a smaller liberal Berber party called the RCD, the communists and others could operate freely again.

The most dramatic change, however, was that Benjedid permitted a new Islamist party to be formed and take part in regular political life.[4] There had not been any Islamic element in Algerian politics since the followers of Ben Bādīs had joined the FLN around 1960. Nor was there any significant Islamist tradition in Algeria. Some intellectuals and religious leaders had argued for greater emphasis on religion and Islamic values, but they were few and had little impact. Thus, the new party had virtually no antecedents and grew out of the circumstances of that moment. It was formed in 1989 under the name of the 'Islamic Salvation Front', FIS.

However, new as it was, the party clearly struck a chord and filled a political lacuna. It was formed in order to participate in the local elections that were promised for the following year, and parliamentary elections in 1991. It grew quickly with local branches all over Algeria. The leadership was dominated by two men who could hardly be more different in background, and who sometimes appeared to diverge fundamentally in politics, but still cooperated closely in building the front. ʿAbbāsī Madanī had a Ph.D. from London and appealed primarily to the middle class. He was a veteran from the liberation war, had participated in the first attacks in 1954 and had been held in French prisons for many years after that. He clearly saw the FIS as a way to return to the ideals of the resistance movement. The other FIS leader and Madanī's second was ʿAlī Belhadj, who was much younger. He was a schoolteacher with no further education, and spoke in much more radical terms than Madanī. His rhetoric found an echo among young Algerians, unemployed or underemployed, but Madanī on several occasions had to 'correct' the statements made by his junior, something that often caused confusion as to what the FIS actually stood for.

They were in favour of Islamic government, but fairly unclear about what that meant. However, they clearly supported Arabization to reduce the French cultural influence, and the position of women was important to them. Algeria had passed a fairly liberal family law in 1981, but this had already been partially reversed already in 1984. The FIS campaigned for a much sharper tightening in line with Sharīʿa rules. These two points brought the front into direct confrontation with two important movements in civil society. The Berber movement, and in particular the small secular RCD, saw that 'Arabizing' meant the Berbers would lose their cultural rights; and the women's movement, which had fought for liberalization in family law, attacked the reactionary nature of the front's proposal.

There was on the whole considerable concern in the modernized and francophone middle class over the intentions of the FIS, in particular their attitude towards democracy. The Front did not help in this by making completely contradictory statements on the issue. Belhadj went far in rejecting 'Western democracy' as un-Islamic and said that secular parties should be banned,[5] while Madanī emphasized that the FIS was firmly grounded in the democratic process and that all parties, including the secular, should have full rights in his Islamic state. Thus, people could choose which of the two they wanted to believe. However, while the party mobilized mass demonstrations, they never moved in the direction of a revolutionary organization. It was clearly meant to be a parliamentary reformist party that worked to achieve its objectives through established institutions.

Benjedid's policy of allowing Islamists to run in elections was completely opposite to that of his neighbours, who all banned or marginalized similar movements. One reason he chose a different path was clearly a tactical evaluation of his position in the political struggle. His basis in the ruling FLN and in the army was weak: both opposed his economic liberalization policy. A medium-sized FIS with a certain electoral basis could balance the FLN, he believed, and thus give him the room to manoeuvre as a middle-man between two equally large political blocks. The FIS did support his economic policies, which also contributed to his tolerance of them.[6]

However, the local elections in 1990 came as a great surprise to everyone. Instead of balancing the FLN, the FIS moved far ahead of it. They gained more than 55 per cent of the popular vote, and took control over two-thirds of the municipalities and regions in the country. There were probably several reasons for this landslide. Certainly, the Islamist agenda genuinely appealed to many voters. But it was also a protest vote against the ruling party, following from the 'bread riots' two years earlier. The FLN was seen as corrupt and incompetent. There were many opposition parties, but most of them boycotted the election and, in any case, they were all composed of former FLN politicians who had jumped ship at one point or another. Only the FIS was a completely new and untainted force without any links to the ruling party, and it was seen as the clearest alternative to the existing system.

Benjedid was not much worried, and withstood the pressure from the FLN to have the FIS banned from parliamentary elections the following year. But he did change the electoral law so that it should be easier for the FLN to keep a majority in Parliament. This enraged the FIS, who organized mass demonstrations in protest. The army was called in and many people were killed in the clashes that followed. Because of this unrest, the leadership of the FIS was arrested in June 1991, and Madanī and Belhadj were both sentenced to several years in prison.

But Benjedid would still not ban the party. A thus weakened FIS would perhaps now get the right number of votes to play the junior role that he envisaged for them. Thus, the parliamentary elections took place as planned with a first round in December 1991, and a run-off planned for January 1992. However, the FIS surprised again. They had shown an impressive ability to regroup and rebuild a leadership, even with the two front figures behind bars. This time, none of the regular parties boycotted this election, but the FIS was still able to garner the highest share of the votes, with 47 per cent of the total. The ruling party, FLN, fell to a dismal third place behind Ait Aḥmad's FFS.

This was not only a surprise, but also meant that the electoral changes Benjadid had made to bolster the largest party (FLN) now instead came to benefit the FIS. They were already close to an overall majority in Parliament after this first round and could aspire to getting a two-thirds majority after the second round of voting. This, however, was it for the military leadership. Since Benjedid was still unwilling to abort the electoral process, they did it for him. The president was deposed in a coup, the elections were cancelled and the FIS dissolved. In the weeks that followed, their party machinery was closed down, and all the municipal representatives elected a year earlier and many regular members of the FIS were arrested; many were sent to prison camps in the Sahara.

This time, the FIS did not recover. Some officials had been able to escape, but the party was in ruins and never came back. Their strategy of winning influence through elections was now blocked. Their suppression left space for more radical forces that promoted a different and more violent strategy.

The situation remained relatively calm for the first year after the coup. The army knew that it had to show willingness to adapt, and brought back the old hero from the liberation war, Muḥammad Boudiaf, and made him President. He had been in exile since 1963 and was therefore unsullied by scandals or taint of corruption. He accepted the post with a programme of reform and promised to clean out the corruption of the previous regime. However, six months later he was assassinated. The crime was never fully clarified, but suspicion was cast both on the Islamists and on circles within the military who disliked Boudiaf's independent style and feared that the anti-corruption campaign would target them. With his death, the army returned to its traditional policies, and the reforms were shelved.

The FIS had obviously not made any contingency plans for the blow that struck them; but there were other Islamist groups that had prepared. There had been some small groups that had advocated and carried out direct action in the 1980s.[7] They had not garnered much support at the time, but their views seemed now to have been vindicated: reforms within the system appeared indeed to be impossible. In the course of 1992 and into 1993 they began attacking police stations and other symbols of government. Their support grew, not least in the municipalities that had voted for the FIS and which the regime now isolated and ignored. In many cases, local Islamist *emirs* took over the practical administration of these isolated communities.[8] Some former FIS members also joined the militant groups. But it was newer and more radical elements that came to dominate them. In 1993, they took the name of the 'Armed Islamic Groups', or GIA.

In addition to attacking the police, the GIA began to pursue civilian targets, in particular intellectuals who were 'enemies of Islam', as well as foreign nationals in Algeria. While the FIS had a broad social basis, the GIA recruited mainly among marginalized social groups, unemployed or otherwise. The more prosperous middle classes that had supported the FIS began to turn against them when the GIA applied pressure to enlist support for their struggle, and resorted to robbery or other crime if the support was not sufficiently forthcoming. Over time, the GIA began to expand its concept of the 'enemy' and became more aggressive against the FIS, whom they now saw as 'infidels' for taking part in the democratic process. They became ever more violent against those they believed did not support them fully, and in particular targeted villages or regions that had voted for the FIS in the elections. The definite shift towards extreme violence came in 1995 when a radical wing took control of the GIA, massacred those former FIS members who had joined the groups in 1992–1993 and began a massive campaign of terror against civilian society, which they branded as generally 'infidel' if it did not actively join or support the GIA.

By 1995, then, Algeria was in reality in a civil war. The regime counter-attacked and was able to capture or kill many of the GIA leaders and dismantle its local groups. But the GIA had a decentralized structure and was able to form new groups in step with the ones the army could destroy. The regime began organizing local counter-terror militias, which they armed and otherwise let loose on the population with the aim of hunting down the GIA wherever it might appear. These militias began their own terror campaign, where the same civilians often became the targets of both sides. Each side that lost a battle or a skirmish could enact revenge on a village they suspected of aiding the other side (under compulsion or not), and respond with killing sprees that could leave whole families dead. The distinction between the terrorists and the counter-terrorists became increasingly blurred and it was often hard to know which side had murdered whom. Often, it was less politics than revenge, with family and clan rivalries being settled under the cover of guerrilla warfare.[9]

The remains of the old FIS quickly saw that they were about to be sidetracked, so organized their own militia, the 'Islamic Salvation Army' or AIS, to harness the frustrations of their supporters. The AIS had a more regional focus in the west and in some areas of the east. It attacked army posts and other government structures and was probably not innocent in targeting civilians. But as the ferocity of the GIA terror grew wilder and approached madness, the AIS stood apart in its political claim that the FIS should be legalized and the results of the 1991 election be recognized. The GIA considered such demands completely irrelevant; only a *jihād*ist state was acceptable to them. Thus, there were of course also clashes between the GIA and the AIS when their groups came into contact.

The regime, now under the presidency of Liamine Zeroual, tried to open talks with the opposition in 1994. The largest traditional parties, such as the FFS and the FLN (which after the coup considered itself a part of the opposition), supported the demands of the ex-FIS that the 1991 elections should be recognized and the FIS legalized. An election without the largest party being allowed to run would be meaningless and have no legitimacy. Other opposition parties, such as the RCD and other strict secularists who became known as the 'eradicators', strongly opposed the suggestion that the 'anti-democratic' FIS should be allowed to play any political role. Zeroual was not able to get around this basic division of views, so the talks never happened. But he did change the regime's economic strategy in 1996. The changes led to a marked improvement in living conditions for most people. At the same time, he proposed an amnesty for guerrillas who were willing to lay down their arms.

These were significant measures, and it was clear that many, perhaps the majority, of those who had voted for the FIS as a form of protest and been neutral in the early years of the conflict now increasingly came to support the government and turn against the guerrillas. The GIA did still recruit young people, but they increasingly relied on terror to enforce support. A number of their fighters deserted and accepted the government's amnesty. This only made the GIA more extreme in their campaigns, and the worst atrocities in the civil war probably took place in 1997–1998, when complete villages were massacred. But the GIA became ever more isolated and it was easier for the army to find the Islamist groups and destroy them, whittling down the guerrillas bit by bit. The war began to wind down from 1999, and the GIA basically no longer existed by 2002. Some smaller legacy groups continued minor attacks and skirmishes, in particular the 'Salafist' group of GSPC, which later took the name 'al-Qāʿida in the Islamic Maghreb'. But the civil war had mostly come to an end by the turn of the millennium.

The AIS had already laid down their arms by 1998. ʿAbd al-ʿAzīz Bouteflika, who had been Foreign Minister under Boumedienne, was elected President unopposed in 1999. He went further in the direction of dialogue and reached an agreement with the AIS, which was disbanded; then he gave a general amnesty to FIS members. Madanī and Belhadj were released from prison in 2003, but were still prevented from any political activity, and the FIS as such remained banned. Some more moderate Islamist parties were allowed to stand in elections, but were unable to take over the FIS electorate. The status of the FIS and the result of the botched multi-party elections of 1990–1991 thus remained unresolved.

Libya: monarchy, oil and Qadhāfi

The smallest of the four countries, Libya, also lived through dramatic changes in the last third of the century. But it was more often international than domestic politics that brought it to the newspaper headlines.

For Libya's first eighteen years of independent existence it remained almost unnoticed by the outside world.[10] The new king, Muḥammad Idrīs al-Sanūsī, came to power in one of the poorest countries in the world with a population of not much more than a million, a corner of the world that few people cared about, notwithstanding its vast, but mostly empty desert territory.[11] When the King fell from power in 1969, Libya was one of the richest countries in the world, and later came to be one about which almost everybody had an opinion.

The first challenge that the new kingdom had to face was that of the relations between its two major regions. The western part, Tripolitania, was reasonably fertile and contained the majority of the population: about two out of three Libyans lived there. But the monarchy was rooted politically in the less populated Cyrenaica. The new elite consisted of tribal leaders and old Sanūsī shaykhs who were close to the King. An attempt to make Benghazi the new capital failed, but the easterners were successful in almost all other ambitions. The government was to be federal, so that Cyrenaica was protected from a Tripolitanian preponderance, while the people in the capital had wanted a unified state. With Fezzan as a separate region, the kingdom thus had three regional governments and administrations in addition to the federal one. The King remained the head of the Sanūsī brotherhood and also tried to rebuild the lodges and the Sanūsī university that had been destroyed by the Italians, but the brotherhood remained mostly restricted to the tribal aristocracy in the east.

Libya was thus a very personal monarchy. It lacked modernized political structures, and it was the traditional tribal leaders who dominated the state. There were no political parties, and parliament and government were composed of notables bound by their loyalty to the King. However, the King did not intervene much in the everyday running of affairs and left those mostly to his ministers, whom he appointed and replaced whenever he wanted.

Things began to change when oil exploration in the 1950s disclosed valuable deposits. Extensive exploitation started in the 1960s and led to an explosion of revenue. The average per capita income was $35 in 1951; $50 in 1960; and in 1968 it was $2,000. By 1979 it had reached almost $10,000.[12] This inevitably changed Libyan society. However, at first the most noticeable result was a large importation of foreign workers, in particular from Egypt, since Libya was unable to raise a sufficient workforce in such a short time.

The king retained close relations with Britain, which had been the mainstay of his international orientation since he became leader of the brotherhood in 1916. It had been the British who had promoted his candidacy as King of Libya, and they were allowed to keep important military bases in Libya, while the USA also had a key airforce base. Relations with France were rather more strained, since France had only reluctantly given up their claims to the Fezzan, which they had governed during and after World War II. The Algerian war did not improve matters, as the King allowed the FLN to operate from Libyan territory. His relationship with Egypt's Nasser and his radical nationalism was however fairly distant. While Libya was part of the Arab community, its support for the 1967 war against Israel was also rather tepid.

By the late 1960s, it was obvious that the traditionalist and fragmented government structures were incapable of dealing with the tremendous changes that Libya went through as oil wealth began to pour in. The kingdom was collapsing from the inside. While the Gulf shaykhdoms were able to adapt their traditional systems to manage the new prosperity, perhaps because they had small and coherent elites, the King had never had more than half-hearted support in the most important region of his kingdom, Tripolitania. The federal system with four governments was clearly inefficient, and in 1963 it was replaced with a unified structure, but without any more fundamental change in monarchic power. King Idrīs was by this time elderly and often ill, and had no obvious successor. The crown Prince was generally considered incompetent, and the King had cut the rest of his family off from succession. As the monarchy thus did not provide any alternative leadership, a coup was expected as the only possible change of government.

The coup that came on 1 September 1969 was thus no great shock, but the direction it came from was a surprise. It was not the top leadership of the army, but a group of subaltern officers with strong ideological motivations that took power. They deposed the King (who was abroad at the time) and declared Libya a republic. These 'free officers' were mostly from the lower middle class and had not been politically active before. However, the coup met no resistance from the army leadership or the political elite, not even in Cyrenaica.

It turned out, after a few days, that the leader of the coup was the young Muʿammar al-Qadhāfī.[13] The coup was technically led by a Revolutionary Council in which ʿAbd al-Salām Jallūd was the dominant personality alongside Qadhāfī, but it was clear from the beginning that Qadhāfī was the undisputed man in charge. He came from a Bedouin family in Sirtica, a district in eastern Tripolitania, and thus was not from the central parts of either of the two large regions. His Bedouin background became very important for him, both in how he presented himself and probably also in reality. He came with a strong empathy for Islam, but with little or no respect for religious scholars, relying instead to a large degree on his own interpretation of the religion.

The new rulers were strongly influenced by Arab nationalism, and Nasser was Qadhāfī's great model. Qadhāfī wanted to put Libya's oil wealth at the service of Nasser and the Arab revolution. This was, however, a bit late in coming; by 1969 Arab socialism had begun to lose its glory, and Nasser died the following year. Qadhāfī thus came to be the last great enthusiast for the ideology that had dominated Arab politics in the 1950s and 1960s.

It is possible to divide the Qadhāfī era into three major periods.[14] In the first five years, the revolution was carried forward by Nasserist enthusiasm and attempts to find a place in the Arab national movement. The Revolutionary Council recognized that it lacked experience in running a country, and first appointed a civilian government. However, within a year the civilian ministers had all been replaced by council members. It established a party, the Arab Socialist Union (taking its name from Nasser's party), which became the only legal party. Foreign banks were closed and the property of the still fairly large Italian community in Libya was nationalized. Together with the large royal domains, this gave the new government resources that it could distribute to new allies.

Foreign policy was aimed at securing and promoting Nasser's ideals of Arab unity. Qadhāfī thus attempted to form a number of unions with neighbouring countries. The first and most serious attempt was to create a 'Federation of Arab States' in 1970–1971, with Egypt, Sudan and Syria. But when Sādāt led Egypt in a direction quite different from that of Nasser's, and relations with Sudan were soured, this idea of an Arab federation collapsed. Later attempts to make unions with Egypt alone (1972–1973), Tunisia (1974), Chad (1981) and Morocco (1984) were equally unsuccessful. Algeria turned down a similar proposal in 1973.

Thus, Qadhāfī had to follow his path alone. He was also in sole and clear control domestically, even though he repeatedly resigned in protest from the Revolutionary Council. From 1973, he began to formulate a more comprehensive ideological base in what he called the 'Third Universal Theory', in the form of a 'Green Book'. The name was of course borrowed from Mao's little red book, and he also lifted some ideas from there. But the universal theory was to be a third path, in contrast to both capitalism and communism and on an Islamic basis. It may in some ways have resembled a vision of utopian socialism with a tinge of anarchism. He attacked Marxism for its focus on classes and the state. Instead of a perennial class conflict, society must build on a partnership between different economic actors. Representative democracy was oppressive; instead, government must be based on direct democracy in local councils.

In the ten years that followed and constituted the second phase of Qadhāfī's rule, attempts were made to reshape Libya after the universal theory. His utopian dislike for the state did not affect the economy, which was completely dominated by state ownership. But local 'popular congresses' were formed to allow all citizens to present their opinions.[15] These congresses then elected regional and national assemblies, but they were not to be 'representatives' but just 'mouthpieces' for the local councils and blindly echo the views expressed there. In reality, this meant that these councils and assemblies had no capacity to make decisions and had no influence on actual policy. That was decided by the Revolutionary Council, which meant Qadhāfī, even though he had in theory 'withdrawn from all power' and left it in the hands of the popular congresses. Following the idea of direct democracy, he also attacked his own party, the ASU, and demanded a 'cultural revolution' there, again a concept borrowed from abroad.

The third universal theory was to be based on Islam. There is no doubt that Qadhāfī was strongly influenced by his religious ideas; this was probably where he most clearly differed from his great mentor, the secularist Nasser. But much of the religious content of his theories was based on his own inspiration and stood in dramatic contrast to the Islam of religious scholars. This class of *ʿulamāʾ* was weak in Libya, but they criticized Qadhāfī for having broken with important elements of the Prophet's *sunna*.

Qadhāfī riposted with a large seminar that he held for the *ʿulamāʾ* in 1978.[16] Islam, he said, was primarily based on God's revelation in the Qurʾān. The *sunna*, the collection of traditions from the Prophet Muḥammad's sayings and doings, was not a good source, because it was written down generations after his death, and much of what it contains were, without doubt, later forgeries. Some Western historians of Islam might agree with him there, but it was a dramatic break with Islamic theology to throw overboard the *sunna*, the most extensive authority for Islamic belief and behaviour. Many in Libya, and even more in other Muslim countries, criticized him with some justification for having broken with Islam, at least with the Islam that the rest of the world knew. Basing one's faith on the solitary source of the Qur'ān without support from the *sunna* opened the religion to all kinds of idiosyncratic interpretations of the text, and it was precisely such idiosyncratic interpretations that were the result.[17]

We can see the effect of this in some remarkable, if symbolic, changes that Qadhāfī made. Most dramatically, he changed the starting point for the Islamic calendar. For everyone else, it begins with the Prophet's emigration from Mecca to Medina in AD 622. But no, Qadhāfī said, this is not the most important date. The turning point must be the end of God's revelation, at Muḥammad's death ten years later in 632. We must count the Islamic era from that year. So while 2011 in the rest of the Muslim world corresponded to the Islamic year 1432, Libya was then in 1422. A similar symbolic measure was to allow only Arabic script to be used in Libyan passports, which caused problems for Libyan nationals travelling to less polyglot corners of the world. The name of the country was also a novelty: instead of the usual term *Jumhūrīya* (state of the people) for 'republic', Libya became a *Jamāhīrīya* (state of the masses), creating an untranslatable neologism in Arabic.

There had not been any popular rebellion behind Qadhāfī's coup, and there was not great enthusiasm for his universal theory. But there was little doubt that his economic and social policies led to a dramatic improvement in the standard of living for most people in the country, and that his intentions to reduce social inequalities were both genuine and put into effect. The government had tremendous resources to pour into these programmes in the golden decade until 1983. Massive housing projects were completed, health and other welfare services were free, and there was an outpouring of subsidised consumer goods. Some people did make more than others, and wealth did end up near the political power centre, but this was overshadowed by the fact that everyone got more. Thus, there is little doubt that Qadhāfī's rule had considerable popular support in this early period, even though all political opposition was ruthlessly suppressed and extensive surveillance searched out any hint of dissent.

But the prosperity was based on one resource alone: oil. Libya has been called a 'distributive state', completely based on the state's access to resources to hand out.[18] This was already the case under the monarchy, which was funded by revenue from the oil companies. Qadhāfī demanded that the Libyan state should become a majority shareholder in all foreign oil companies, but still allowed the foreign owners a minority of the shares. When some companies refused, they were nationalized completely. This transfer of ownership was implemented at the same time as oil prices rose rapidly from 1973, and marked the apex of Libyan oil wealth.

The crash came in 1983, the same crisis that brought about the problems in Algeria. Libya had fewer inhabitants and more oil, so the effects were not so dire here. But the state's revenue fell from 21 billion dollars in 1982 to only 5 billion in 1986, and this inevitably had an impact on society. The government had great problems in maintaining levels of social welfare, and consumer goods began to disappear from shops as prices reached unattainable levels.

The economic crisis led to a political reorientation in 1986–1987. The government dropped many of the more utopian ideas of the 1970s, and 'normalized' many aspects of government. Economic liberalization opened up easier imports of food and other consumer goods, so that the queues disappeared. Some political reforms were also instituted, the revolutionary committees were disbanded, Libyans were allowed to travel freely abroad, and some political prisoners were released. However, Qadhāfī still had a colourful way to illustrate the changes: he rode a bulldozer to 'tear down' Tripoli's main prison. There was, however, still 'no need' for an independent press or different parties in the 'mass state'.

Libya also tried to ease tensions abroad, after having been considered a pariah state for years.[19] After his early emphasis on

Arab nationalism and failed attempts at unity, he turned his attention southwards to Africa. He developed a great interest in the internal affairs of various African countries and was often accused of interfering in local conflicts with arms or even soldiers, but also funded some countries generously. Thus, he was given credit for the transformation of the older Organization of African Unity into the African Union in 2002.

He also tried to mend fences with the Western powers. However, progress here was slow. The US still considered Libya as one of the world's foremost promoters of terrorism; not without reason, as Qadhāfī had given generous support to a varied bouquet of radical groups around the world. He had financed Palestinian leftist groups that opposed 'Arafāt (with whom Qadhāfī had quarrelled), the Venezuelan terrorist Carlos, the IRA in Northern Ireland and the Green Party in Germany (some said because of their party colour). The conflict with the Western powers was exacerbated when US planes bombed Qadhāfī's house in Tripoli in 1986 and killed his adoptive daughter. Three years later, Libya was accused of blowing up an American passenger aircraft over Lockerbie in Scotland, and Western countries refused to deal with Libya until this affair was settled. Libya accepted responsibility for the attack only in 1999, after which the diplomatic climate thawed to some degree.

The US and Western countries were also aware that Qadhāfī was a sharp enemy of the growing Islamist movement. His rule had now become a completely secular one in which the Green Book was more important than Islamic traditions. The only real opposition within Libya came from some Islamist students in Benghazi; however, they were easily crushed and appeared to be isolated. Still, Qadhāfī saw this as a warning signal and severely suppressed any tendencies in an Islamist direction. Thus, the old 'supporter of international terrorism' became an ally to the US in the 'war against terrorism'.

The basic features of Qadhāfī's rule remained, but much of the early utopianism had dwindled away after a generation. The system was still centred around the personal rule of Qadhāfī, in spite of him having no other title than 'Brother, leader of the revolution'. Rising oil prices in the 1990s also helped to stabilize his reign and stave off pressures for more radical changes in his system.

8

NORTH AFRICA TOWARDS A NEW AGE?

The four countries along the southern shore of the Mediterranean have taken different paths through history. But there have also been marked similarities, in particular between the two that were protectorates, Tunisia and Morocco, but also between the two that were not, Algeria and Libya.[1] They have also, after independence, tended to go in two directions in international politics, Tunisia and Morocco generally 'moderate' and close to the Western powers, while Libya under Qadhāfī and Algeria have had 'radical' regimes and closer contact with the Soviet Union.

This has also marked their domestic policies. The two radical countries, which have also been the richest in oil, have promoted Arab socialism with a strong state sector, while the two others have promoted liberal capitalism to a greater degree. However, this division was never quite clear cut. Tunisia had its socialist period in the 1960s, and the economy there too dominated by a strong public sector. And Qadhāfī even in his most radical period, always preserved private ownership in the oil sector. But it does indicate that oil wealth gave the state in Algeria and Libya more freedom to influence economy and society than in the other two countries.

Oil also made them more sensitive to fluctuations in the world market oil prices, and both moved away from state control towards economic, and a budding political, liberalization in the 1980s, more so in Algeria than in Libya. The fall of the Soviet bloc also made a realignment of foreign policy necessary, and the distinction between 'radical' and 'moderate' became less pronounced and partly disappeared. This was also instrumental in bringing the four countries closer and opened the way for greater cooperation between them.[2]

Qadhāfī's Libya was clearly the most insistent on cooperation with other countries. However, positioned on the border between the Maghreb and the Mashreq, Libya was as much interested in contacts eastwards towards Egypt or south to Africa as with the other three Maghreb countries, who shared a history of French dominance, language and culture. They have a common past, with or without Tripolitania, going back to ages long before the Arab conquest, and it was natural for the independent countries also to try to bind together in some form of formal cooperation.

However, it must be said that the efforts have not borne much fruit. The high point of Maghreb cooperation was probably the 1950s, when all three independent countries supported the FLN's struggle and let them operate from their territory, in spite of the conflicts with France that this caused.

But when all were free, there was little consensus. In fact, there were border disputes between all countries that shared a frontier. Typically, it was the two countries which had the most distinct pre-colonial history, Morocco and Tunisia, that demanded territories from their younger neighbours. Such disputes often concerned desert regions with few if any inhabitants and without any clear identity or border demarcation before the colonial period, and where France had not bothered to be too precise in drawing its colonial borders. Tunisia demanded some areas on its southern fringe from Algeria and some from Libya. Libya also demanded some areas further south in the Sahara from Algeria. Most of these conflicts were solved by negotiations, however, and the borders were in all cases left as they had been at independence.

Libya had also, as early as in 1954, claimed territories in the south from the French colony of Chad. This concerned a small and uninhabited stretch of land in the middle of the Sahara without any resources, the Aouzou strip. The claim went unheeded, but was brought up again by Qadhāfī in the 1970s.[3] Chad was of particular interest to him because some of the populations in northern Chad and southern Libya were ethnically related. He supported various rebel movements in northern Chad, and in 1972 he used the occasion to send in troops to claim the formerly disputed area. It took more than twenty years before a decision in the International Court of Justice in 1994 established that this border was also to remain as it had been during the colonial period, and the Libyan troops left the area.

However, the conflicts in the west were of greater consequence. There were several disputes. Morocco and Algeria both claimed a desert region, the two oases of Tindouf on the Algerian side and Figuig on the Moroccan, and fought a brief 'sand war' over them just after Algerian independence. Again, the border remained as it had been, and Morocco shelved its claims, but never formally accepted the frontier.

Mauritania between West Africa and the Maghreb

It was areas to the south, however, that caused most concern. Morocco had the longest history in the Maghreb as a separate state, and claimed that all tribes southwards to the Senegal and Niger rivers had historically accepted the sovereignty of the Moroccan sultan. Thus, when the French colonial empire was dissolved in the late 1950s, they felt that Morocco's historical boundaries had to be re-established. This concerned some sections of French Soudan, which became Mali, but primarily the French colony that became the republic of Mauritania. Morocco insisted that all of it was part of historical Morocco.

Mauritania was a desert region virtually without any arable land, with a population mostly of nomads in some oasis towns and a few fishing villages on the coast. The dominant tribes spoke an Arabic dialect called Ḥassānīya.[4] There was also a West African population which spoke various African languages, many of whom were of servile origin or still lived as slaves or serfs.[5]

French forces had occupied this area in 1903, but had only been able to overcome nomadic resistance in the mid 1930s.[6] The French were not particularly interested in it since it had few resources, but still administered it as a separate entity within French West Africa (AOF). As the French were pulling back from their colonies in the 1950s, a small elite of Mauritanians had been involved in the colonial administration, but were also closely integrated in the traditional tribal structure.

There was some disagreement among the leaders of the new republic as to whether Mauritania should direct its attention southwards and become a part of West Africa or focus on its links to the Arab north in the Maghreb. The Ḥassānīya-speaking groups naturally looked to the north, but did not see attachment to Morocco as an alternative. One Mauritanian leader did however go to Rabat and supported the Moroccan King's claim. But a party led by Mukhtār Wuld Daddah won general approval, and he became the republic's first President. He tried to find a balance between north and south, and thus Mauritania came to see itself both as a part of sub-Saharan Africa and of the Maghreb.

It had been the old nationalist hero ʿAllāl al-Fāsī who had most vociferously fought for the Moroccan annexation of Mauritania. The claim was not considered unreasonable by Morocco's neighbours, and the Algerian FLN, Libya, Egypt and other Arab countries all supported Morocco in its demand. Only Tunisia sided with Mauritania. The majority vote in the UN, however, went in favour of recognizing Mauritania's independence, and it was thus accepted as a part of the Maghreb, although Morocco only finally recognized it in 1969. Soon after, the two countries would stand united in the struggle over another almost unpopulated part of the western desert.

The Sahara conflict

Through Spain's search for protectorates, it had occupied not only part of northern Morocco, but also more extensive regions to the south. In addition to the small enclave of Sidi Ifni that it had won in the war in 1860, it also 'protected' a strip of land called Tarfaya, which international agreements considered as an undisputed part of Morocco; this area was returned to Morocco in 1958.

However, the areas further south had no clear owner or identity. They consisted of two desert regions called Ṣaqīyat al-Ḥamrā' and Wādī Dhahab (Rio del Oro).[7] The Spanish had established trading posts in the 1880s in two small towns, Villa Cisernos and al-ʿAyūn, to cater for the many fishers who sought the rich waters off the coast; but the hinterland, as far as anyone knew, was without any exploitable resources. An agreement in 1912 delimited the Spanish territories from the French AOF to the south and east, and Morocco to the north.

When Franco died in 1974, the democratic government that followed wanted to dismantle the remains of the Spanish colonial empire, and thus leave Spanish Sahara. Morocco immediately posted its claim to the territory, due to its historical and geographic contiguity. But, at the same time, a 'Front for the liberation of Ṣaqīyat al-Ḥamrā' and Rio del Oro', Polisario, appeared and demanded independence for the region, supported by Algeria.

It was difficult to sort out the various historical claims to the region, as it had never had any specific identity in the past. No borders, of course, had ever been drawn in the desert between the pre-modern rulers, so arguments had to be made from what the peoples of that time had believed: thus who they had paid tax or tribute to or acknowledged as their sovereign. Of course, this was hampered by the fact that such tax or tribute payments had always been reluctantly paid and had varied from generation to generation or even from year to year. However, a central figure in the history of Western Sahara, just at the onset of colonialism, was the Sufi resistance leader Muṣṭafā al-Fāḍilī, known as Mā' al-ʿAynayn.[8] He established a centre for his Fāḍilīya brotherhood at Smāra in Ṣaqīyat al-Ḥamrāʾ in 1880, but also owned property in southern Morocco. As French troops arrived from the south, he organized the resistance in Mauritania and is considered as one of the greatest heroes of this region. He was also close to the Moroccan sultans. Sultan ʿAbd al-ʿAzīz had funded him, but he had supported the rival ʿAbd al-Ḥafīẓ when the latter criticized French influence in the country. But when ʿAbd al-Ḥafīẓ became Sultan, he turned against the unruly Māʾ al-ʿAynayn, who tried unsuccessfully to raise a revolt against the new Sultan.

The Moroccans claimed that Māʾ al-ʿAynayn had acted with the support of the Sultan, as his agent, and that he had made the Saharan tribes accept the Sultan's authority. Those who opposed Morocco's claim to Western Sahara insisted that the rebel had worked on his own and had only asked for the Sultan's support when they were both threatened by a common enemy, the French. A possible answer could be that both may be right, and that there was no great distinction between the two attitudes in the mind of the actors in 1910, any more than there had been for ʿAbd al-Qādir in 1840.

The Spanish were pressed for time in leaving the Sahara, and shortly after the 'green march' in 1975 accepted a tripartite agreement with Morocco and Mauritania, whereby the two countries split the territory. Morocco took the northern and Mauritania the southern part. However, Polisario had strong international and diplomatic backing.[9] Many African states saw the movement as a continuation of their own struggle for decolonization, and supported Polisario's demand for an independent state. African states were also generally reluctant to accept changes in the colonial borders. Thus, when Polisario declared a new Democratic Arab Saharan (Ṣahrawī) Republic in 1976, it was recognized by the majority of African states and given a seat in the Organization of African Unity (OAU). Morocco left the OAU and broke diplomatic connections with all states that recognized the new republic. This has left Morocco isolated in African politics ever since.

Polisario started guerrilla warfare with Algerian support, and made significant advances in the first few years; but Morocco retained full control over the Saharan population centres on the coast. Mauritania, however, was not able to keep the Polisario forces at bay, so they made peace with Polisario and recognized the Saharan republic. Morocco immediately took over the territory that Mauritania had left, and has since considered all of the former Spanish colony as an integral part of Morocco.

This was not just a matter of national honour and some empty stretches of Saharan sand. In addition to the exceptionally rich fishing resources, the area turned out to have the largest deposits of phosphate in the world. Closest in rank is Morocco, and the two combined completely dominate the world market in phosphates.

Polisario made Tindouf, an oasis just across the border in Algeria, their centre, and many refugees from the fighting came there. Morocco had trouble in defeating the Polisario forces in the large desert tracts. But by 1980–1982 they had constructed a large sand wall that protected the phosphate mines and the populated centres, and they were able to hold this wall. Polisario continued to operate east of it, but from the 1980s no longer constituted any military threat to Morocco. Algeria has also diplomatically moved closer to Morocco, and has accordingly reduced its support for Polisario.

The conflict remained unresolved, however. The UN and the US have worked for a referendum to settle the issue of independence or integration into Morocco, but the parties could not agree on who would be allowed to vote—Morocco moved many immigrants into the Sahara, which complicated the issue—and the referendum never took place.

The Arab Maghreb Union

In spite of the historical ties and an undisputable feeling of togetherness, the many conflicts and rivalries between the Maghreb countries have weakened most attempts at cooperation.[10] For long periods of time some of the Maghreb states have not even had diplomatic relations with others, and there has hardly been any trade between them. Often, the main regional contacts have been through a third party and, economically, particularly through the relations that each of them have with the European Union. Some attempts were made to forge a joint Maghrebi approach or treaty with the EU, but these attempts failed.[11]

Some of the regional tension was relaxed in the course of the 1980s, and in 1989 all five—Morocco, Algeria, Tunisia, Libya and Mauritania—agreed to establish the 'Arab Maghreb Union'. This was, unlike Qadhāfī's many unity projects, to be limited to economic cooperation before any political structures could be envisaged, following the model of the history of the European Economic Community in the 1950s and 1960s. The five countries should remove their customs barriers and work towards a unified budgetary strategy and a common currency, and eventually also work towards coordinating foreign policy.

This cooperation never got far beyond the planning stage, because of disagreements over the Sahara issue and the civil war that broke out in Algeria, but it represented a stronger intent to work as a region than had been seen in the preceding decades. However, the greatest force for integration was probably the EU and the treaties that each of these countries negotiated with the European body, which may have the effect of promoting cooperation also between the Maghreb states.

The Arab Spring

In the winter of 2011, a wave of demonstrations for more democracy, less corruption and improved social conditions swept over the Arab world. The movements had many sources: they were partly spurred by a deteriorating economy after the world financial crisis, but also inspired by the spread of political ideas through new social media, not least among educated middle-class youth. The demands were similar from country to country; but the events that followed were quite different in each.

The whole movement sparked off in Tunisia in December 2010, when a street vendor set himself on fire in frustration over police harassment. This led to large protests, which came to focus on President Ben ʿAlī and his family, who were accused of rampant corruption. Even though Tunisia had a high standard of living compared with many neighbouring countries, it also suffered from the harsh oppression of political opposition. It was not a military dictatorship—Tunisia had always had civilian rule—but the police were instrumental in quelling any dissent.

In spite of attempts to crush them, in which about 100 participants were killed, demonstrations continued in Tunis and other major cities, demanding Ben ʿAlī's resignation. He gave in after a month and left the country on 14 January. A transitional government took over until new elections could be held. The ruling RCD party, which had been in power under different names since independence in 1956, was disbanded. New liberal opposition parties were formed, and Rashīd Ghannūshī, leader of the Islamist al-Nahḍa party, returned from exile. When elections were held at the end of 2011, al-Nahḍa, as expected, became the largest party and sought a coalition with several liberal parties.

There were also demonstrations for democracy in Algeria, at about the same time as in Tunisia. However, these were quelled fairly easily by the police. Bouteflika's regime responded with economic reforms that benefited many sectors in society, and this seemed to be sufficient to stave off further widespread protest.

The protest movement was also fairly moderate in Morocco, but it continued throughout the spring. Here the demonstrations were mostly tolerated, unlike in most Arabic countries, and they did not become serious clashes, although some protesters were killed here as well. The demand was not that the king should resign, but that he should democratize the government and make Morocco a constitutional monarchy. The king accepted some of the demands and a revised constitution was passed, stating that the Prime Minister and government should now be appointed by a majority in parliament, rather than by the King personally, as had been the case. But the King retained his personal control over the military, foreign policy and some other areas. The democracy movement considered this insufficient, but the reforms appeared to be enough to prevent further revolts.

The most dramatic events took place in Libya. Demonstrations for a regime change very quickly turned violent when they began in February, one month after the first victory in Tunisia. The demonstrations spread quickly across the country, but had their greatest strength in Cyrenaica. This eastern part of Libya felt ignored under Qadhāfī, who disliked and feared it because of its history as a backbone of the old monarchy. The regime struck back with great ferocity and more than 300 protesters were killed by police and armed forces in the first three days alone. Some army elements in Benghazi rebelled and, aided by protesters, took over the military barracks and raided many weapon depots. In many towns in the east, as well as in the west, the police and army simply disappeared, and the demonstrators suddenly found themselves in charge of 'liberated zones'. After some time, the regime was able to consolidate its forces and reconquer most of the towns in Tripolitania that had been lost; only the coastal town of Miṣurāta, east of Tripoli, and the Jabal Nafūsa mountains towards the Tunisian border remained in rebel hands. But all of Cyrenaica fell to the rebels, who made Benghazi their headquarters.

The government forces began an advance towards the east, and by the middle of March were close to Benghazi when NATO forces mandated by the UN intervened with air attacks on the regime's troops and forced them into retreat. With foreign intervention restricted to air support, the rebels were able to hold Cyrenaica but not move forward, and the war was protracted through spring and summer. By August, however, the rebels were able to break through from Jabal Nafūsa and conquered Tripoli, thus ending Qadhāfī's 42-year reign. Qadhāfī himself was caught and killed three months later. The new transitional council promised elections but, as in the other Arab states, the revolution did not answer every question about which type of regime would replace the old.

The Maghreb has thus, in these last two centuries, moved from an epoch where the eastern three-quarters were under the formal rule of Istanbul, through an epoch where the western three-quarters were under the effective rule of Paris, to a present where independent states are trying to find a regional identity. This history has had a great effect on how these countries develop. Tunisia and Morocco have in many ways shared parallel paths, already differing from the other Maghrebi territories before 1800, in that they were 'countries' with separate identities and a concept of internal cohesion, while the others were modern constructions. In both Algeria and Libya a 'national identity' had to be created through modern protagonists such as the FLN, around which Algeria's modern identity has largely been formed. In Libya, Qadhāfī was perhaps the only common focus for an identity that may now be shattered.

The similarity between Tunisia and Morocco can also be seen in the period of French rule, when the traditional political system in both cases was integrated into the new, and the old ruling class was given a role to play, even though a subsidiary one (unlike in Algeria). Their softer transition into colonialism was repeated in a softer transition out of colonial rule into independence. In Morocco, it was the traditional royal power that came back in a modernized form. In Tunisia, the bey disappeared and a new political class replaced his rule in a clearer modernist break with the past. But the change here was also pacific and gradual; while the two other countries, Algeria and Libya, were both liberated through war. There, the modern political systems were formed through a sharp break with the past (in Libya by the coup in 1969), and therefore they were also dominated by military rule, since the military was the single cohesive element in the new social structure.

The Maghreb is a part of the Arab and Islamic world and an integral part of the larger 'Middle East'. But its heritage and geographic cohesion mean that it will also find its own path and have its own characteristics within this larger community.

NOTES

INTRODUCTION

1. Pinar Bilgin, 'Inventing Middle Easts? The Making of Regions Through Security Discourses', in B.O. Utvik and K.S. Vikør (eds.), *The Middle East in a Globalized World*, Bergen 2000, 10–38.

1. THE GROWTH OF THE MUSLIM MAGHREB

1. Jamil M. Abun-Nasr, *A History of the Maghrib in the Islamic Period*, Cambridge 1987, and Charles-André Julien, *Histoire d'Afrique du Nord. Des origines à 1830*, Paris 1994.
2. Hugh Kennedy, *Muslim Spain and Portugal: A Political History of al-Andalus*, London 1996, 1–30.
3. Tadeusz Lewicki, 'La répartition géographique des groupements ibāḍites dans l'Afrique du nord au moyen-âge', *Rocznik Orientalistyczny*, xxi, 1957, 301–43, and *idem*, 'The Ibádites in Arabia and Africa', *Cahiers d'histoire mondial*, xiii, 1971, 51–130.
4. Ulrich Rebstock, *Die Ibāḍiten im Maġrib (2./8.-4./10. Jh.): Die Geschichte einer Berberbewegung im Gewand des Islam*, Berlin 1983; Elizabeth Savage, *A Gateway to Hell, a Gateway to Paradise: The North African Response to the Arab Conquest*, Princeton 1997; and Virginie Prevost, *L'aventure ibāḍīte dans le Sud tunisien (VIIIe–XIIIe siècle): Effervescence d'une région méconnue*, Helsinki 2008.
5. Roger le Tourneau, *Fès avant le protectorat: Étude économique et sociale d'une ville de l'occident musulman*, Casablanca 1949, 25–92.
6. Abun-Nasr, *History of the Maghrib*, 53–9; and Julien, *Histoire d'Afrique du Nord*, 380–9.

7. Farhad Daftary, *The Ismāʿīlīs: Their History and Doctrine*, Cambridge 1990, 144–255; Heinz Halm, *The Empire of the Mahdi: the Rise of the Fatimids*, Leiden 1996; Michael Brett, *The Rise of the Fatimids: The World of the Mediterranean and the Middle East in the Fourth Century of the Hijra, Tenth Century CE*, Leiden 2001; and Prevost, *L'aventure ibāḍīte*, 113–54.
8. H.T. Norris, *The Berbers in Arabic Literature*, London 1982, 105–56; Vincent Lagardère, *Les almoravides,* Paris 1989, 1998; Kennedy, *Muslim Spain and Portugal*, 154–88, and Ronald A. Messier, *The Almoravids and the Meanings of Jihad*, Santa Barbara 2010.
9. Abun-Nasr, *History of the Maghrib*, 87–103; Allen J. Fromherz, *The Almohads: The Rise of an Islamic Empire*, London 2010; and Maribel Fierro, *The Almohad Revolution: Politics and Religion in the Islamic West during the Twelfth-Thirteenth Centuries*, Aldershot 2012.
10. Mercedes García-Arenal, *Messianism and Puritanical Reform, Mahdīs of the Muslim West*, Leiden 2006, 157–92.
11. Abun-Nasr, *History of the Maghrib*, 118–34; and Julien, *Historie d'Afrique du Nord*, 489–511.
12. H.T. Norris, *The Arab Conquest of the Western Sahara*, London 1986.
13. Mohamed Kably, *Société, pouvoir et religion au Maroc à la fin du Moyen-Age*, Paris 1986; Ahmed Khaneboubi, *Les premiers sultans Mérinides (1269–1331): Histoire politique et sociale*, Paris 1987; and Maya Shatzmiller, *The Berbers and the Islamic State: The Marīnid Experience in Pre-Protectorate Morocco*, Princeton 2000. For the role of religious models for Moroccan dynasties, see García-Arenal, *Messianism and Puritanical Reform*, 217–95.
14. Abun-Nasr, *History of the Maghrib*, 206–19; and Julien, *Histoire d'Afrique du nord,* 571–88.
15. John O. Hunwick, *Timbuktu and the Songhay Empire: Al-Saʿdī's Taʾrīkh al-Sūdān Down to 1613 and Other Contemporary Documents*, Leiden 1999; and Richard L. Smith, *Ahmad al-Mansur: Islamic visionary*, New York 2006.
16. Ernest Gellner, *Saints of the Atlas*, Chicago 1969; and Vincent J. Cornell, *Realm of the Saint. Power and Authority in Moroccan Sufism*, Austin, TX 1998.
17. Abun-Nasr, *History of the Maghrib*, 228–47; and Julien, *Histoire d'Afrique du nord*, 594–616.
18. Patricia Mercer, 'Palace and jihād in the early ʿAlawī state in Morocco', *Journal of African History*, xviii, 4, 1977, 531–53.
19. Jerome Bookin-Weiner, 'Corsairing in the economy and politics of North Africa', in George Joffé (ed.), *North Africa: Nation, State and Region*, London 1993, 3–33.
20. Abun-Nasr, *History of the Maghrib*, 144–68; and Julien, *Histoire d'Afrique du nord*, 625–53.
21. Julien, *Histoire d'Afrique du nord*, 653–94.

22. Jacques Berque, *L'intérieur du Maghreb, xve-xixe siècle*, Paris 1978.
23. Eugène Vayssettes, *Histoire de Constantine sous la domination turque de 1517 à 1837*, Paris 2002.
24. Abun-Nasr, *History of the Maghrib*, 179–82.
25. Robert Brunschvig, 'Justice religieuse et justice laïque dans la Tunisie des Deys et des Beys jusqu'au milieu du xixe siècle', in *Études d'islamologie*, Paris 1976.
26. Ettore Rossi, *Storia di Tripoli e della Tripolitania: Dalla conquista araba al 1911*, Rome 1968, 221–58.
27. On the size and importance of one important item, see John Wright, *The Trans-Saharan Slave Trade*, London 2007.
28. Knut S. Vikør, *Sufi and Scholar on the Desert Edge: Muḥammad b. ʿAlī al-Sanūsī and his Brotherhood*, London 1995.
29. Le Tourneau, *Fès avant le protectorat*, 453–80.
30. Rachid Abdalla El-Nasser, 'Morocco from Kharijism to Wahhabism: The Quest for Religious Purism', Ph.D., University of Michigan 1983, and *Sufi and Scholar*, 35–40.
31. Arnold H. Green, 'A Tunisian Reply to a Wahhabi Proclamation: Texts and Contexts', in A.H. Green (ed.), *In Quest of an Islamic Humanism. Arabic and Islamic Studies in Memory of Mohamed al-Nowaihi*, Cairo 1984, 155–77; and Mohamed El Mansour, *Morocco in the Reign of Mawlay Sulayman*, Wisbech 1990, 138–43.
32. El-Mansour, *Morocco in the Reign of Mawlay Sulayman*, 89–90.
33. Bradford G. Martin, *Muslim Brotherhoods in Nineteenth-Century Africa*, Cambridge 1976, 43–5; Mehdi Bouabdelli, 'Documents inédits sur la révolte des Derqâwa en Oranie', in J. Berque and D. Chevallier (eds.), *Les Arabes par leurs archives*, Paris 1976, 93–100; and Vikør, *Sufi and Scholar*, 53–8.
34. Abun-Nasr, *History of the Maghrib*, 180–7.
35. Rossi, *Storia di Tripoli e della Tripolitania*, 259–94; and Kọla Fọlayan, *Tripoli during the Reign of Yūsuf Pāshā Qaramānlī*, Ile-Ife 1979.
36. Ḥabīb Wadāʿa El-Ḥesnāwī, *Fazzān under the rule of the Awlād Muḥammad*, Sabha 1990.
37. Dennis D. Cordell, 'The Awlad Sulayman of Libya and Chad: Power and Adaptation in the Sahara and the Sahel', *Canadian Journal of African Studies*, 2, 1985, 319–43.

2. THE FRENCH INVASION OF ALGERIA

1. For a study of how everyday life was in the Maghreb in the late pre-colonial period, see Lucette Valensi, *On the Eve of Colonialism: North Africa before the French Conquest*, New York 1977.

2. Charles-Robert Ageron, *Modern Algeria: A History from 1830 to the Present*, London 1991, 5–12; and Raphael Danziger, *Abd al-Qadir and the Algerians: Resistance to the French and Internal Consolidation*, New York 1977, 36–50.
3. Charles-André Julien, *Histoire de l'Algérie contemporaine*, Paris 1979, i, 68–71, 81–2; and Ageron, *Modern Algeria*, 6.
4. Amira K. Bennison, *Jihad and its Interpretations in Pre-colonial Morocco: State-Society Relations during the French Conquest of Algeria*, London 2002, 48–58.
5. Danziger, *Abd al-Qadir and the Algerians*, 51–63; and Bruno Étienne, *Abdelkader: Isthme des isthmes*, Paris 1994, 129–30.
6. Danziger, *Abd al-Qadir and the Algerians*, 71–179.
7. Raphael Danziger, 'Abd al-Qadir and Abd al-Rahman: Religious and Political Aspects of Their Confrontation (1843–1847)', *Maghreb Review*, vi, 1–2, 1981, 27–35; and Bennison, *Jihad and its Interpretations*, 75–157.
8. Danziger, *Abd al-Qadir and the Algerians*, 89–94; and Ageron, *Modern Algeria*, 9–13.
9. Jamil M. Abun-Nasr, *The Tijaniyya: A Sufi Order in a Modern World*, London 1965, 62–8.
10. Étienne, *Abdelkader*, 192–212; and Bennison, *Jihad and its Interpretations*, 106–13.
11. Bennison, *Jihad and its Interpretations*, 33–41.
12. C.R. Pennel, *Morocco Since 1830: A History*, London 2000, 41–9; and Bennison, *Jihad and its Interpretations*, 99–131.

3. THE MAGHREB BECOMES FRENCH: 1850–1912

1. Julia A. Clancy-Smith, *Rebel and Saint: Muslim Notables, Populist Protest, Colonial Encounters (Algeria and Tunisia 1800–1904)*, Berkeley 1994.
2. Allan Christelow, *Muslim Law Courts and the French Colonial State in Algeria*, Princeton 1985.
3. Thus, most of British-ruled Africa was administered through the Colonial Office, the ministry for the colonies, while the areas they dominated in the Middle East, even the Sudan, fell under the Foreign Office.
4. Ageron, *Modern Algeria*; Julien, *Histoire de l'Algérie contemporaine*; and Benjamin Stora, *Histoire de l'Algérie coloniale (1830–1954)*, Paris 1991, 25–40.
5. In Algeria, the term 'Muslim' is often used to denote the non-French, not necessarily because religion was the main identifier, but because saying 'Arab' hides the important Berber element of the population. 'Muslim' covers both.
6. Tuomo Melasuo, 'The Problems and Contradictions of Land Conflicts in Algeria', in H. Palva and K.S. Vikør (eds.), *The Middle East Viewed from the North*, Bergen 1992, 85–92.

7. Stora, *Algeria, 1830–2000: A Short History*, Ithaca 2001, 7 (cf. his *Histoire de l'Algérie coloniale*, 23).
8. Cf. for example the seminal studies of Sufism in Algeria by Louis Rinn, *Marabouts et Khouan. Étude sur l'Islam en Algérie*, Alger 1884; and Octave Depont and Xavier Coppolani, *Les Confréries musulmanes*, Paris 1897, among many others.
9. Ageron, *Modern Algeria*, 72–3. For a later sociological study of Kabyle Berbers, see Pierre Bourdieu's texts in *Algeria*, Cambridge 1979, 95–153. Among Algeria's Berber-speaking peoples should also be mentioned the Tuareg of the far south; the effects of colonialism and independence on their society is described by Jeremy Keenan in *The Tuaregs*, London 1977, and *The Lesser Gods of the Sahara*, London 2004.
10. Pennel, *Morocco*, 40–174.
11. Edmund Burke III, *Prelude to Protectorate in Morocco: Precolonial Protest and Resistance, 1860–1912*, Chicago 1976.
12. For a recent study of the trade, cf. Ghislaine Lydon, *On Trans-Saharan Trails, Islamic Law, Trade Networks, and Cross-cultural Exchange in Nineteenth-century Western Africa*, Cambridge 2009.
13. Kenneth L. Brown, *People of Salé: Tradition and Change in a Moroccan City, 1830–1930*, Manchester 1976; and Pennel, *Morocco*, 68–87.
14. Abdallah Laroui, *Esquisses historiques*, Casablanca 1992, 63–72.
15. Id., *Les Origines sociales et culturelles du nationalisme marocain (1830–1912)*, Casablanca 1993.
16. Burke, *Prelude to Protectorate*, 41–7.
17. Ross E. Dunn, *Resistance in the Desert: Moroccan Responses to French Colonialism 1881–1912*, London 1977, 231–58.
18. Pennel, *Morocco*, 160–3.
19. Martin, *Muslim Brotherhoods*, 125–51.
20. Lyautey moved Morocco's capital from Fez to Rabat in 1912.
21. L. Carl Brown, *The Tunisia of Ahmad Bey: 1837–55*, Princeton, NJ 1974.
22. Lisa Anderson, *The State and Social Transformation in Tunisia and Libya, 1830–1980*, Princeton 1986, 57–113.
23. Albert Hourani, *Arabic Thought in the Liberal Age 1798–1939*, Cambridge 1962, 84–95; and G. S. van Krieken, *Khayr al-Dîn et la Tunisie (1850–1881)*, Leiden 1976, 146–272.

4. THE PROTECTORATES AND NATIONALISM

1. Pennel, *Morocco*, 160–3.
2. Pessah Shinar, '‘Abd al-Qādir and ‘Abd al-Krīm: Religious Influences on their Thought and Action', *Studies in Islam*, July 1964, 135–64.

3. Hourani, *Arabic Thought*, 130–60.
4. Laroui, *Esquisses historiques*, 123–46, and Mohamed El Mansour, 'Salafis and Modernists in Morocco's Nationalist Movement', in John Ruedy (ed.), *Islamism and Secularism in North Africa*, New York 1996, 53–69.
5. Pennel, *Morocco*, 242–53.
6. Claire Spencer, 'The Spanish Protectorate and the Occupation of Tangier in 1940', in Joffé, *North Africa*, 91–104.
7. Kenneth J. Perkins, *Modern History of Tunisia*, Cambridge 2004, 10–38.
8. Arnold H. Green, *The Tunisian Ulama 1873–1915: Social Structure and Response to Ideological Currents*, Leiden 1978.
9. Perkins, *Modern History of Tunisia*, 73–129.
10. Perkins, *Modern History of Tunisia*, 89–104; and Anderson, *State and Social Transformation*, 167–78.
11. Perkins, *Modern History of Tunisia*, 110–29.

5. ARMED RESISTANCE

1. Ali Abdullatif Ahmida, *The Making of Modern Libya: State Formation, Colonization and Resistance, 1830–1932*, Albany, NY 1994, 103–40; and John Wright, *Libya: A Modern History*, London 1983, 25–43.
2. E.E. Evans-Pritchard, *The Sanusi of Cyrenaica*, Oxford 1949; and Vikør, *Sufi and Scholar*.
3. Jean-Louis Triaud, *La Légende noire de la Sanûsiyya. Une confrérie musulmane saharienne sous le regard français (1840–1930)*, Paris 1995.
4. G.F. Abbott, *The Holy War in Tripoli*, London 1912; and Knut S. Vikør, '*Jihād*, *ʿilm* and *taṣawwuf*—two justifications of action from the Idrīsī tradition', *Studia Islamica*, xc, 2000,153–76.
5. Cf. various contributions to E.G.H. Joffé and K.S. McLahlan (eds.), *Social and Economic Development of Libya*, London 1982, 43–159.
6. Evans-Pritchard, *Sanusi*, 134–41.
7. Enzo Santarelli et al., *Omar al-Mukhtar. The Italian Reconquest of Libya*, London 1986.
8. Wright, *Libya*, 25; and Angelo Del Boca, *Gli italiani in Libia*, Rome 1986.
9. Wright, *Libya*, 44–59; and Dirk Vandevalle, *A History of Modern Libya*, Cambridge 2006, 34–40.
10. Ageron, *Modern Algeria*, 65–81.
11. Michael Willis, *The Islamist Challenge in Algeria: A Political History*, London 1996, 1–35.
12. Ageron, *Modern Algeria*, 96–7.
13. Benjamin Stora, *Histoire de la guerre d'Algérie (1954–1962)*, Paris 1992.

6. INDEPENDENCE: AUTHORITY AND MODERNITY

1. Anderson, *State and Social Transformation*, 231–50; and Perkins, *Modern History of Tunisia*, 130–56.
2. Lars Rudebeck, *Party and People: A Study of Political Change in Tunisia*, Uppsala 1967.
3. For a study of family and women's rights in the modern Maghreb, see particularly Mounira M. Charrad, *States and Women's Rights: The Making of Postcolonial Tunisia, Algeria, and Morocco*, Berkeley 2001. For the Tunisian reform, see pp. 201–32.
4. Maud Eduards, *Samarbete i Maghreb*, Stockholm 1985.
5. Christopher Alexander, *Tunisia: Stability and Reform in the Modern Maghreb*, Milton Park 2010, 68–88.
6. Mohamed Elhachmi Hamdi, *The Politicisation of Islam: A Case Study of Tunisia*, Boulder, CO 1998.
7. Emma C. Murphy, *Economic and political change in Tunisia: from Bourguiba to Ben Ali*, Basingstoke 1999. Bourguiba sometimes claimed to have been born in 1901, which would have made him 99 at his death, but the later birth date appears to be better attested.
8. Pennel, *Morocco*, 299–309.
9. Pennel, *Morocco*, 324–30.
10. Tony Hodges, *Western Sahara: The Roots of a Desert War*, Westport, CT 1983.
11. François Burgat, *The Islamic Movement in North Africa*, Austin, TX 1993, 136–52; and Okacha Ben Elmostafa, *Les Mouvements islamiques au Maroc. Leurs modes d'action et d'organisation*, Paris 2007.
12. He was a member of the Bouchichiya brotherhood, typical for its modern and middle-class membership, but broke with it in the 1980s; Malika Zeghal, *Islamism in Morocco. Religion, Authoritarianism and Electoral Politics*, Princeton 2008, 77–142.
13. Léon Buskens, 'Recent Debates on Family Law Reform in Morocco: Islamic Law as Politics in an Emerging Public Sphere', *Islamic Law and Society*, x, 1, 2003, 70–131.
14. Anouar Boukhars, *Politics in Morocco. Executive Monarchy and Enlightened Authoritarnianism*, London 2011.

7. STATES AND IDEOLOGIES: ALGERIA AND LIBYA

1. William B. Quandt, *Revolution and Political Leadership: Algeria, 1954–1968*, Cambridge, MA 1969; and Stora, *Algeria*.
2. Marc Raffinot and Pierre Jacquemot, *Le Capitalisme d'état algérien*, Paris 1977.

3. Salem Mezhoud, 'Glasnost the Algerian Way: The Role of the Berber Nationalists in Political Reform', in Joffé, *North Africa*, 142–69.
4. Willis, *Islamist Challenge*, 107–56; and Luis Martinez, *La Guerre civile en Algérie. 1990–1998*, Paris 1998 (trans. *The Algerian Civil War*, London 2000).
5. Mustafa al-Ahnaf, Bernard Botiveau and Franck Frégosi (eds.), *L'Algérie par ses islamistes*, Paris 1991, 84–98.
6. Hugh Roberts, 'Doctrinaire economics and political opportunism in the strategy of Algerian Islamism', in Ruedy, *Islamism and Secularism in North Africa*, 123–48.
7. Willis, *Islamist Challenge*, 70–94.
8. Martinez, *Guerre civile*, 119–88.
9. Among the many accounts of these events, see e.g. Abed Charef, *Algérie: Autopsie d'un massacre*, La Tour d'Aigues 1998; and Baya Gacemi, *Moi, Nadia, femme d'un émir du GIA*, Paris 1998.
10. Wright, *Libya*, 77–118; and Vandewalle, *History of Modern Libya*, 43–76.
11. J.A. Allan (ed.), *Libya Since Independence: Economic and Political Development*, London/New York 1982.
12. Dirk Vandewalle, *Libya Since Independence: Oil and State-building*, Ithaca 1998, 50.
13. Ruth First, *Libya: The Elusive Revolution*, Harmondsworth 1974; Jonathan Bearman, *Qadhafi's Libya*, London 1986; and Ronald Bruce St John, *Libya. Continuity and Change*, Milton Park 2011, 48–142.
14. Vandewalle, *History of Modern Libya*.
15. Studies on the local politics in Libya under Qadhāfi include John Davis, *Libyan Politics: Tribe and Revolution: An Account of the Zuwaya and their Government*, London 1987; and Amal Obeidi, *Political Culture in Libya*, London 2001.
16. Mahmoud Ayoub, *Islam and the Third Universal Theory. The Religious Thought of Muʿammar al Qadhdhafi*, London 1987, 74–88.
17. Marius K. Deeb, 'Militant Islam and its critics: The case of Libya', in Ruedy, *Islamism and secularism*, 187–97; and Goerge Joffé, 'Qadhafi's Islam in Local Historical Perspective', in Dirk Vandewalle (ed.), *Qadhafi's Libya: 1969 to 1994*, New York 1995, 139–53.
18. Vandewalle, *Libya Since Independence*, 17–38.
19. Vandewalle, *History of Modern Libya*, 139–206.

8. NORTH AFRICA TOWARDS A NEW AGE?

1. Benjamin Stora, 'Algeria/Morocco: The passions of the past. Representations of the nation that unite and divide', in James McDougall (ed.), *Nation, Society and Culture in North Africa*, London 2003, 14–34.

2. Eduards, *Samarbete i Maghreb.*
3. Bernard Lanne, *Tchad-Libye. La querelle des frontières*, Paris 1982, 227–34; and John Wright, *Libya, Chad and the Central Sahara*, London 1989, 126–46.
4. Norris, *Arab Conquest.*
5. Urs Peter Ruf, *Ending Slavery: Hierarchy, Dependency and Gender in Central Mauritania*, Bielefeld 1999.
6. Geneviève Désiré-Vuillemin, *Histoire de la Mauritanie: Des origines à l'indépendance*, Paris 1997. Studies on pre-colonial and early colonial Mauritania include Charles C. Stewart, *Islam and Social Order in Mauritania: A Case Study from the Nineteenth Century*, Oxford 1973; Abdallah Ould Khalifa, *La Région du Tagant en Mauritanie. L'oasis de Tijigja entre 1660 et 1960*, Paris 1998; and David Robinson, *Paths of Accommodation: Muslim Societies and French Colonial Authorities in Senegal and Mauritania, 1880–1920*, Athens, OH 2000, 161–93.
7. Ali Omar Yara, *Genèse politique de la société sahraouie* (*L'Ouest Saharien*, HS 1), Paris 2001.
8. Martin, *Muslim Brotherhoods*, 125–51; and Rahal Boubrik, *Saints et sociétés en islam: La confrérie ouest saharienne Fâdiliyya*, Paris 1999.
9. Elsa Assidon, *Sahara occidental: Un enjeu pour le nord-ouest africain*, Paris 1978; and Toby Shelley, *Endgame in the Western Sahara: What future for Africa's Last Colony?* London 2004.
10. Samir Amin, *The Maghreb in the Modern World*, Harmondsworth 1970; and Eduards, *Samarbete.*
11. Ali Bahaijoub, 'Morocco's arguments to join the EEC'; and John Damis, 'The Maghreb Arab Union and regional reconciliation'; both in Joffé, *North Africa*, pp. 235–46, 288–96.

BIBLIOGRAPHY

Maghreb in general

Abun-Nasr, Jamil M., *A History of the Maghrib in the Islamic Period*, Cambridge 1987.

Amin, Samir, *The Maghreb in the Modern World*, Harmondsworth 1970.

Berque, Jacques, *Le Maghreb entre deux guerres*, Paris 1962, 1967; trans. *French North Africa: The Maghrib Between Two World Wars*, New York 1962.

———, *L'intérieur du Maghreb, xve-xixe siècle*, Paris 1978.

Bilgin, Pinar, 'Inventing Middle Easts? The Making of Regions Through Security Discourses', in B.O. Utvik and K.S. Vikør (eds.), *The Middle East in a Globalized World*, Bergen 2000, 10–38.

Burgat, François, *The Islamic Movement in North Africa*, Austin, TX 1993.

Charrad, Mounira M., *States and Women's Rights: The Making of Postcolonial Tunisia, Algeria, and Morocco*, Berkeley 2001.

Daftary, Farhad, *The Ismāʿīlīs: Their History and Doctrine*, Cambridge 1990.

Eduards, Maud, *Samarbete i Maghreb*, Stockholm 1985.

Fierro, Maribel, *The Almohad Revolution: Politics and Religion in the Islamic West during the Twelfth-Thirteenth Centuries*, Aldershot 2012.

Gellner, Ernest and Charles Micaud (eds.), *Arabs and Berbers*, London 1973.

Halm, Heinz, *The Fatimids and Their Tradition of Learning*, London 1997.

Hourani, Albert, *Arabic Thought in the Liberal Age 1798–1939*, Cambridge 1962.

Joffé, George (ed.), *North Africa: Nation, State and Region*, London 1993.

Julien, Charles-André, *Histoire d'Afrique du Nord. Des origines à 1830*, Paris 1951, repr. 1994; trans. *History of North Africa: Tunisia, Algeria, Morocco from the Arab Conquest to 1830*, London 1970.

Lagardère, Vincent, *Les Almoravides*, Paris 1989, 1998.

Laroui, Abdallah, *L'Histoire du Maghreb: Un essai de synthèse*, Paris 1970; trans. *The History of the Maghrib, An Interpretive Essay*, Princeton 1977.

Lewicki, Tadeusz, 'La répartition géographique des groupements ibāḍites dans l'Afrique du nord au moyen-âge', *Rocznik Orientalistyczny*, xxi, 1957, 301–43.

———, 'The Ibádites in Arabia and Africa', *Cahiers d'histoire mondial*, xiii, 1971, 51–130.

Martin, Bradford G., *Muslim Brotherhoods in Nineteenth-Century Africa*, Cambridge 1976.

McDougall, James (ed.), *Nation, Society and Culture in North Africa*, London 2003.

Mernissi, Fatima, *Le Harem politique. Le Prophète et les femmes*, Paris 1987.

———, *The Forgotten Queens of Islam*, Cambridge 1993.

Morsy, Magali, *North Africa 1800–1900. A Survey from the Nile Valley to the Atlantic*, London 1984.

Norris, Harry T., 'New Evidence on the Life of ʿAbdullāh b. Yāsīn and the Origins of the Almoravid Movement', *Journal of African History*, xii, 2, 1971, 255–68.

———, *The Berbers in Arabic Literature*, London 1982.

Rebstock, Ulrich, *Die Ibāḍiten im Maġrib (2./8.-4./10. Jh.): Die Geschichte einer Berberbewegung im Gewand des Islam*, Berlin 1983.

Ruedy, John (ed.), *Islamism and Secularism in North Africa*, New York 1996.

Savage, Elizabeth, *A Gateway to Hell, a Gateway to Paradise: The North African Response to the Arab Conquest*, Princeton 1997.

Valensi, Lucette, *On the Eve of Colonialism: North Africa before the French Conquest*, New York 1977.

Wright, John, *The Trans-Saharan Slave Trade*, London 2007.

Morocco

Abun-Nasr, Jamil M., *The Tijaniyya: A Sufi Order in a Modern World*, London 1965.

Ben Elmostafa, Okacha, *Les Mouvements islamiques au Maroc. Leurs modes d'action et d'organisation*, Paris 2007.

Bennison, Amira K., *Jihad and its Interpretations in Pre-colonial Morocco: State-Society Relations during the French Conquest of Algeria*, London 2002.

Boukhars, Anouar, *Politics in Morocco. Executive Monarchy and Enlightened Authoritarnianism*, London 2011.

Brown, Kenneth L., *People of Salé: Tradition and Change in a Moroccan City, 1830–1930*, Manchester 1976.

Burke, Edmund III, *Prelude to Protectorate in Morocco: Precolonial Protest and Resistance, 1860–1912*, Chicago 1976.

Buskens, Léon, 'Recent Debates on Family Law Reform in Morocco: Islamic Law as Politics in an Emerging Public Sphere', *Islamic Law and Society*, x, 1, 2003, 70–131.

Cornell, Vincent J., *Realm of the Saint. Power and Authority in Moroccan Sufism*, Austin, TX 1998.

Dunn, Ross E., *Resistance in the Desert: Moroccan Responses to French Colonialism 1881–1912*, London 1977.

García-Arenal, Mercedes, *Messianism and Puritanical Reform, Mahdīs of the Muslim West*, Leiden 2006.

Geertz, Clifford, *Islam Observed: Religious Development in Morocco and Indonesia*, Chicago 1971.

Gellner, Ernest, *Saints of the Atlas*, Chicago 1969.

Halstead, John, *Rebirth of a Nation: The Origins and Rise of Moroccan Nationalism, 1912–1944*, Cambridge, MA 1967.

Hunwick, John O., *Timbuktu and the Songhay Empire: Al-Saʿdī's Taʾrīkh al-Sūdān Down to 1613 and Other Contemporary Documents*, Leiden 1999.

Kably, Mohamed, *Société, pouvoir et religion au Maroc à la fin du Moyen-Age*, Paris 1986.

Khaneboubi, Ahmed, *Les premiers sultans Mérinides (1269–1331): Histoire politique et sociale*, Paris 1987.

Jackson, James Grey, *An Account of the Empire of Morocco: and the Districts of Suse and Tafilelt*, London 1814.

Laroui, Abdallah, *L'Idéologie arabe contemporaine: Essai critique*, Paris 1967.

———, *Esquisses historiques*, Casablanca 1992.

———, *Les Origines sociales et culturelles du nationalisme marocain (1830–1912)*, Casablanca 1993.

Lévi-Provençal E., *Les Historiens des chorfas: Essai sur la littérature historique et biographique au Maroc du xvie au xxe siècle*, Paris 1922.

Lydon, Ghislaine, *On Trans-Saharan Trails, Islamic Law, Trade Networks, and Cross-Cultural Exchange in Nineteenth-Century Western Africa*, Cambridge 2009.

El Mansour, Mohamed, *Morocco in the Reign of Mawlay Sulayman*, Wisbech 1990.

Mercer, Patricia, 'Palace and jihād in the early ʿAlawī State in Morocco', *Journal of African History*, xviii, 4, 1977, 531–53.

El-Nasser, Rachid Abdalla, 'Morocco from Kharijism to Wahhabism: The Quest for Religious Purism', Ph.D., University of Michigan 1983.

Pennel, C.R., *Morocco Since 1830: A History*, London 2000.

Shatzmiller, Maya, *The Berbers and the Islamic State: The Marīnid Experience in Pre-Protectorate Morocco*, Princeton 2000.

Smith, Richard L., *Ahmad al-Mansur: Islamic Visionary*, New York 2006.

Tourneau, Roger le, *Fès avant le protectorat: Étude économique et sociale d'une ville de l'occident musulman*, Casablanca 1949.

Zeghal, Malika, *Islamism in Morocco. Religion, Authoritarianism and Electoral Politics*, Princeton 2008.

BIBLIOGRAPHY

Algeria

Ageron, Charles-Robert, *Modern Algeria: A History from 1830 to the Present*, London 1991.

al-Ahnaf, Mustafa, Bernard Botiveau and Franck Frégosi (eds.), *L'Algérie par ses islamistes*, Paris 1991.

Bouabdelli, Mehdi, 'Documents inédits sur la révolte des Derqâwa en Oranie', in J. Berque and D. Chevallier (eds.), *Les Arabes par leurs archives*, Paris 1976, 93–100.

Bourdieu, Pierre, *Algeria 1960*, Cambridge 1979.

Charef, Abed, *Algérie: Autopsie d'un massacre*, La Tour d'Aigues 1998.

Christelow, Allan, *Muslim Law Courts and the French Colonial State in Algeria*, Princeton 1985.

Clancy-Smith, Julia A., *Rebel and Saint: Muslim Notables, Populist Protest, Colonial Encounters (Algeria and Tunisia 1800–1904)*, Berkeley 1994.

Danziger, Raphael, *Abd al-Qadir and the Algerians: Resistance to the French and Consolidation*, New York 1977.

———, 'Abd al-Qadir and Abd al-Rahman: Religious and Political Aspects of their Confrontation (1843–1847)', *Maghreb Review*, vi, 1–2, 1981, 27–35.

Depont, Octave and Xavier Coppolani, *Les Confréries musulmanes*, Paris 1897.

Duveyrier, Henri, *Les Touareg du Nord: Exploration du Sahara*, Paris 1864.

Étienne, Bruno, *Abdelkader: Isthme des isthmes (Barzakh al-barazikh)*, Paris 1994.

Gacemi, Baya, *Moi, Nadia, femme d'un émir du GIA*, Paris 1998.

Julien, Charles-André, *Histoire de l'Algérie contemporaine*, 2 vols., Paris 1979.

Keenan, Jeremy, *The Tuareg: People of Ahaggar*, London 1977.

———, *The Lesser Gods of the Sahara*, London 2004.

Lamchichi, Abderrahim, *L'islamisme en Algérie*, Paris 1992.

Martinez, Luis, *La Guerre civile en Algérie 1990–1998*, Paris 1998; trans. *The Algerian Civil War*, London 2000.

Melasuo, Tuomo, 'The Problems and Contradictions of Land Conflicts in Algeria', in H. Palva and K.S. Vikør (eds.), *The Middle East Viewed from the North*, Bergen 1992, 85–92.

Quandt, William B., *Revolution and Political Leadership: Algeria, 1954–1968*, Cambridge, MA 1969.

Raffinot, Marc and Pierre Jacquemot, *Le Capitalisme d'état algérien*, Paris 1977.

Rinn, Louis, *Marabouts et Khouan. Étude sur l'Islam en Algérie*, Alger 1884.

Shinar, Pessah, "Abd al-Qādir and 'Abd al-Krīm: Religious Influences on their Thought and Action', *Studies in Islam*, July 1964, 135–64.

Stora, Benjamin, *Histoire de l'Algérie coloniale (1830–1954)*, Paris 1991.

———, *Histoirede la guerre d'Algérie (1954–1962)*, Paris 1992.

———, *Histoire de l'Algérie depuis l'indépendance*, Paris 2006, trans. *Algeria, 1830–2000: A Short History*, Ithaca 2001.

Vayssettes, Eugène, *Histoire de Constantine sous la domination turque de 1517 à 1837*, Paris 2002.

Willis, Michael, *The Islamist Challenge in Algeria: A Political History*, London 1996.

Tunisia

Abdelmoula, Mahmoud, *Jihad et colonialisme: La Tunisie et la Tripolitaine (1914–1918). De la guerre sainte à la guerre juste*, Tunis 1987.

Alexander, Christopher, *Tunisia: Stability and Reform in the Modern Maghreb*, Milton Park 2010

Anderson, Lisa, *The State and Social Transformation in Tunisia and Libya, 1830–1980*, Princeton 1986.

Brown, L. Carl, *The Tunisia of Ahmad Bey: 1837–55*, Princeton, NJ 1974.

Brunschvig, Robert, 'Justice réligieuse et justice laïque dans la Tunisie des Deys et des Beys jusqu'au milieu du xixe siècle', in Brunschvig, *Études d'islamologie*, Paris 1976.

Green, Arnold H., *The Tunisian Ulama 1873–1915: Social Structure and Response to Ideological Currents*, Leiden 1978.

———, 'A Tunisian Reply to a Wahhabi Proclamation: Texts and Contexts', in A.H. Green (ed.), *In Quest of an Islamic Humanism. Arabic and Islamic Studies in Memory of Mohamed al-Nowaihi*, Cairo 1984, 155–77.

Hamdi, Mohamed Elhachmi, *The Politicisation of Islam: A Case Study of Tunisia*, Boulder, CO 1998.

Martin, Jean-François, *La Tunisie de Ferry a Bourguiba*, Paris 1993.

Murphy, Emma C., *Economic and Political Change in Tunisia: from Bourguiba to Ben Ali*, Basingstoke 1999.

Perkins, Kenneth J., *A Modern History of Tunisia*, Cambridge 2004.

Prevost, Virginie, *L'aventure ibāḍite dans le Sud tunisien (VIIIe–XIIIe siècle): Effervescence d'une région méconnue*, Helsinki 2008.

Rudebeck, L., *Party and People: A Study of Political Change in Tunisia*, Uppsala 1967.

Valensi, Lucette and Abraham L. Udovitch, *Juifs en terre d'Islam: les communautés de Djerba*, Paris 1984.

van Krieken, G.S., *Khayr al-Dîn et la Tunisie (1850–1881)*, Leiden 1976.

Libya

Abbott, G.F., *The Holy War in Tripoli*, London 1912.

Ahmida, Ali Abdullatif, *The Making of Modern Libya: State Formation, Colonization and Resistance, 1830–1932*, Albany, NY 1994.

Allan, J.A. (ed.), *Libya Since Independence: Economic and Political Development*, London/New York 1982.

Ayoub, Mahmoud, *Islam and the Third Universal Theory. The Religious Thought of Muʿammar al Qadhdhafi*, London 1987.

Baldinetti, Anna (ed.), *Modern and Contemporary Libya: Sources and Historiographies*, Rome 2003.

Bearman, Jonathan, *Qadhafi's Libya*, London 1986.

Cordell, Dennis D., 'The Awlad Sulayman of Libya and Chad: Power and Adaptation in the Sahara and the Sahel', *Canadian Journal of African Studies*, 2, 1985, 319–43.

Davis, John, *Libyan Politics: Tribe and Revolution: An Account of the Zuwaya and their Government*, London 1987.

Del Boca, Angelo, *Gli italiani in Libia*, 2 vols., Rome 1986–8.

Duveyrier, Henri, *La Confrérie musulmane de Sîdi Mohammed Ben 'Alî es-Senoûsî et son domaine géographique en l'année 1300 de l'hégire = 1883 de notre ère*, Paris 1884.

Evans-Pritchard, E.E., *The Sanusi of Cyrenaica*, Oxford 1949.

First, Ruth, *Libya: The Elusive Revolution*, Harmondsworth 1974.

Fọlayan, Kọla, *Tripoli during the Reign of Yūsuf Pāshā Qaramānlī*, Ile-Ife 1979.

El-Ḥesnāwī, Ḥabīb Wadāʿa, *Fazzān under the Rule of the Awlād Muḥammad. A Study in Political, Economic, Social and Intellectual History*, Sabha 1990.

Joffé, E.G.H. and K.S. McLahlan (eds.), *Social and Economic Development of Libya*, London 1982.

Lanne, Bernard, *Tchad-Libye. La querelle des frontières*, Paris 1982.

Obeidi, Amal, *Political Culture in Libya*, London 2001.

Peters, Emrys L., *The Bedouin of Cyrenaica. Studies in Personal and Corporate Power*, Cambridge 1990.

Rossi, Ettore, *Storia di Tripoli e della Tripolitania: Dalla conquista araba al 1911*, Rome 1968.

Santarelli, Enzo et al., *Omar al-Mukhtar. The Italian Reconquest of Libya*, London 1986.

St John, Ronald Bruce, *Libya. Continuity and Change*, Milton Park 2011.

Triaud, Jean-Louis, *La Légende noire de la Sanûsiyya. Une confrérie musulmane saharienne sous le regard français (1840–1930)*, 2 vols., Paris 1995.

Vandewalle, Dirk (ed.), *Qadhafi's Libya: 1969 to 1994*, New York 1995.

———, *Libya Since Independence: Oil and State-building*, Ithaca 1998.

———, *A History of Modern Libya*, Cambridge 2006.

Vikør, Knut S., *Sufi and Scholar on the Desert Edge: Muḥammad b. ʿAlī al-Sanūsī and his Brotherhood*, London 1995.

———, '*Jihād, ʿilm* and *taṣawwuf*—two justifications of action from the Idrīsī tradition', *Studia Islamica*, xc, 2000, 153–76.

Wright, John, *Libya: A Modern History*, London 1983.

———, *Libya, Chad and the Central Sahara*, London 1989.

Sahara

Assidon, Elsa, *Sahara occidental: Un enjeu pour le nord-ouest africain*, Paris 1978.

Boubrik, Rahal, *Saints et sociétés en islam: La Confrérie ouest saharienne Fâdiliyya*, Paris 1999.

Désiré-Vuillemin, Geneviève, *Histoire de la Mauritanie: Des origines à l'indépendance*, Paris 1997.

Hodges, Tony, *Western Sahara: The Roots of a Desert War*, Westport, CT 1983.

Jus, Christelle, *Soudan français-Mauritanie, une géopolitique coloniale (1880–1963): Tracer une ligne dans le désert*, Paris 2003.

Norris, Harry T., *The Arab Conquest of the Western Sahara: Studies of the historical events, religious beliefs and social customs which made the remotest Sahara a part of the Arab world*, London 1986.

Ould Khalifa, Abdallah, *La Région du Tagant en Mauritanie. L'oasis de Tijigja entre 1660 et 1960*, Paris 1998.

Robinson, David, *Paths of Accommodation: Muslim Societies and French Colonial Authorities in Senegal and Mauritania, 1880–1920*, Athens, OH 2000.

Ruf, Urs Peter, *Ending Slavery: Hierarchy, Dependency and Gender in Central Mauritania*, Bielefeld 1999.

Shelley, Toby, *Endgame in the Western Sahara: What future for Africa's Last Colony?* London 2004.

Stewart, Charles C., *Islam and Social Order in Mauritania: A Case Study from the Nineteenth Century*, Oxford 1973.

Yara, Ali Omar, *Genèse politique de la société sahraouie* (*L'Ouest Saharien*, HS 1), Paris 2001.

INDEX